Marketing and Selling Your ●●● Handmade Jewelry

Marketing and Selling Your Handmade Jewelry

The Complete Guide to Turning Your Passion into Profit

VIKI LAREAU

INTERWEAVE PRESS

INTERWEAVE PRESS
201 East Fourth Street
Loveland, CO 80537-5655 USA
www.interweave.com

Printed and bound in China through Asia Pacific Offset.

Library of Congress Cataloging-in-Publication Data
Lareau, Viki, 1965-
    Marketing and selling your handmade jewelry : the complete guide to
turning your passion into profit / Viki Lareau, author.
        p. cm.
    Includes bibliographical references and index.
    ISBN 13: 978-1-59668-024-1 (pbk.)
    ISBN 10: 1-59668-024-5 (pbk.)
    1. Beadwork. 2. Jewelry making. I. Title.
    TT860.L39 2006
    745.594'20688--dc22
                                    2006010572

10 9 8 7 6 5 4 3 2 1

This book is dedicated to my wonderful husband, Mark, and our three children, Trevor, Julian, and Sophia. All the business success in the world wouldn't mean anything without you.

Acknowledgments

Writing this book was the most fun I have had in a long time; it also was the hardest thing I've done in a long time. Since the book is based on a class I've taught for years, I really thought it was going to be a piece of cake—but I did not consider how much cake I would consume through stress eating. You wouldn't think it would be possible to eat while you're writing, but I am an outstanding multitasker, if nothing else.

I have lots of folks to thank for this opportunity. First is my editor, Linda Ligon, who (as I have told her), is the most accomplished woman I have ever known. I am so blessed to have her in my life—thanks for encouraging me so much.

Thanks to Interweave Press for also taking this chance on this book. Everyone there has always been so much help—I really appreciate our family there.

Thank you to my amazing girls at The Bead Factory. My staff makes our store and my life run smoother every day. I love you girls to the bottom of my heart; you are my village and I will always be here for you.

Thanks to all my wonderful customers, without whom none of this would be possible, for all the years of support. I only hope we have given you as much joy as you have brought to our lives. I hope we all continue to inspire and encourage one another for many years to come.

Finally, I want to thank my amazing husband, Mark. We are each other's biggest fans. It means more than I can ever say to have someone in my life who is always in my corner. I'm thankful you hung in there long enough for me to get what that means. I love you.

Contents

Preface: My Story

I'm often asked how in the world I got into the business of beads and jewelry making. It's a long story, but here's the *Reader's Digest* condensed version.

I was studying fashion marketing in college and working part-time in the jewelry department at Nordstrom. Everyone in my family worked for Nordstrom and I knew I would, too. All I ever wanted to do was to be a buyer for this icon of retailing in the Pacific Northwest.

I was offered a management position while I was still in school, so I promptly dropped out, to my mother's dismay. It wasn't long before I was transferred to a chain of stores called Place Two, Nordstrom's younger, hipper version of itself. When those stores closed, instead of transferring somewhere else in the company, I took a management job for a small bead store in Seattle. Since corporate life hadn't been the fantasy I imagined, I thought it was time for a change. I figured I could always go back.

Shortly after I took that job, the company, Beadworks (which had three stores at the time), was bought out by a gentleman in Vancouver, British Columbia. His ambition was to open stores all across Canada, and I moved to Vancouver to help him. I worked on site locations, fitting out the stores, hiring and training, and merchandising. We opened seventeen stores in the three years I was there. About a year into this process, my boss hired a very good-looking boy from Montreal to do all the importing. I promptly snatched him up and we started dating. Apparently he hadn't heard about aggressive American girls (or maybe he had!). Mark and I were married almost a year to the day after we met and had our first child just a year later.

At the time Trevor was born, I was traveling about three weeks out of each month. After his birth I didn't want to keep the same schedule. The owner and I couldn't come to an agreement on that point, so I quit on the spot and told him that Mark was quitting, too. I then informed Mark that we had quit our jobs and were going to open our own store. We had already had many fantasy conversations about this, but I don't think either of us thought it would ever really happen. But I knew just the place.

I grew up in the small town of Enumclaw, just east of Seattle, where my mom still lives. I called her to tell her of our new plans. Then I asked if we

(and our new baby) could move home with her, and if we could borrow $10,000 to open the store. She's a very generous woman, but not a rich one, and she had to borrow against her house to loan us the money.

We opened our first store in Tacoma in September 1992. It was 300 square feet, the rent was $400 a month, and on our first day we sold $192 worth of beads. We were thrilled! Our success continued and we quickly outgrew that space and moved to 700 square feet just six months later. Then we opened a second store, in Seattle. Now we had the rent, payroll, and taxes of two stores, and we got pregnant again. This time we were blessed with twins. However, about halfway through the pregnancy I was put on bed rest. Expenses piled up faster than we could pay them. Mark was trying to run two stores and take care of a two-year-old. The real kicker was that celebrities suddenly stopped wearing jewelry. Why does this matter? My business, like yours, is based on fashion. Paying attention to the trends and keeping ahead of them is how to win the game. I didn't catch it until it was too late. We were deep in financial trouble.

While we were blessed with two beautiful new babies, our business was dying. We had cars repossessed, we almost lost our house, and at any given time our power, water, or phone would be turned off. Creditors calling day and night, and pleading with the bank to float us another day, was our reality.

Mark at work in his shop

But we vowed to turn it around. We closed our Seattle store and laid off most of our employees. Mark and I took turns working in our Tacoma store and staying home with the kids, alternating every day. It was your day off if you got to go to the store!

We didn't want to do anything else. I knew I had the product and the customer service down. It was the lack of business knowledge that was killing us. So we put together a new plan. We started offering innovative classes, doing shows all over the country, and putting every penny back into new inventory. We made an aggressive plan to get out of debt, and we paid cash for every expense so we didn't incur new debt. We worked twelve-hour days, every day. There was literally blood, sweat, and tears in building it all back. We surprise ourselves with how much we are willing to endure when we're passionate about something.

There's no magic ending, no happily ever after. Not in business. Today we have 5,000 square feet, twenty employees, multimillion dollar sales, and lots of expenses. We still put in long days, do not incur new debt, and invest every bit back into the business, though these days it's likely to go toward employee perks or upgraded computer systems (and the occasional pair of Manolo Blaniks, which I consider a business expense).

Viki with beads and computer—multitasking!

I love everything about this business and am grateful to the bottom of my soul for our experiences. Two steps forward and one step back is still progress.

—*Viki Lareau*

Introduction: How It All Begins

Jewelry—I don't know a woman on the planet who doesn't love it. People from every culture have adorned themselves since the beginning of time. Be it through rituals, ceremonies, or gifts, jewelry has been a token of love that we give one another or ourselves to express our feelings.

But making jewelry—that starts differently for everyone. Having owned a bead and jewelry-making supply store for almost fifteen years, I have had the privilege of seeing many artists' beginnings. I've watched hundreds of peoples' lives change. Beading and making jewelry can be a pivotal part of that process, whether it's from the therapeutic value of making something beautiful or by turning this passion into a business.

My own business has never been about selling beads but about delivering an experience—creating a place where a person can relax, surround herself with beauty, and explore her creative side with guidance (which is where I come in). This has always been my passion and why I have never sold my own jewelry in a serious way. But I have had the joy of teaching and guiding hundreds of jewelry makers by helping them selling their work.

Getting into this business starts the same way for most people. You're in Costco, or at church, or at work, and someone says, "That's a beautiful necklace." You smile shyly and say "Oh, thank you—I made it." Then they say, "You did! Do you sell your work? How much would it be? Could you make me one in blue?" Well, you don't want to sound like you don't know how much your own work cost you to make (even though you don't), so you invent some underpriced amount. Your brand-new customer comes back a week later and says, "My sister loves that bracelet, and can you make one for my friend, too?" And then maybe it happens again, and again. Pretty soon, you start to think, "Hey maybe I could really do this!"

Your mind starts to explore a lot of possibilities—selling part-time at shows on weekends for a little extra income, or selling just enough to support your bead addiction. (There's nothing wrong with that!) Or maybe your regular job is seasonal, so you could do shows in your off season. Maybe you're thinking about some supplemental income for your upcoming retirement, or maybe you want to quit your job and do this full time! The world is your oyster, Baby!

What's so cool about being an independent jewelry maker is that you can do it on any of those levels. You can start as small as you like and grow slowly, or you can invest a bunch of money and start big. You might get a lot of accounts and employees and decide it's too much and adjust the business back down to a smaller scale. I don't know many other kinds of work where you have that kind of freedom and flexibility. You can work from home or around family, and your income is completely unlimited and depends solely on how much time and effort you're willing to invest.

I have based this book on a class I've taught all over the country for the past ten years, "The Business of Jewelry." I also do private business consulting for jewelry designers and bead store owners. Finding success, as I've seen many people do, is a journey. This book is about taking that journey, one step at a time. So no matter where you are along this path, whether you are just thinking about getting into it or have been selling your work for years, I ask you to start at the beginning and thoroughly examine what it takes to be successful in the business of jewelry making. I think it's hard to get somewhere you haven't been before without a map, so I hope that's what this book will be for you.

The world of handmade jewelry is always exciting, always changing, always challenging. Jewelry styles and trends may change, but there will always be a market for it. I invite you to explore this passionate side of you and see what beauty emerges.

One. First Steps

Before you make the big leap into selling your own work in a serious way, there's a lot of dreaming and soul-searching to be done. Making basic decisions to build a business on is a little bit like doing psychoanalysis on yourself. It requires self-examination and brutal honesty—about your goals, your personal style, your limitations, your wants and needs. But coming up with a vision that is all your own is the basis for everything that comes later.

The lifestyle—are you cut out for it?

The first thing you need to think about is whether the life of an independent artist/businessperson suits you. There's a common misconception about working at home—robe, slippers, a little Oprah. Can you be your own boss when no one is watching? Here are some important questions to ask yourself:

*   *Are you self-motivated?* Can you get the job done without a supervisor guiding you? Can you stay stimulated by the work itself when there is no one else around? As peaceful as it can be, working for yourself at home can get quite lonely.
*   *Do you have a private space to work?* Just about everyone starts at their dining room table, but this is probably not the ideal work environment when you're ready to get serious, even if you have another place to

serve meals. Really, you need a space to call your own. This might be a spare bedroom, attic, or basement area, but even just an extra table or gutted-out closet can work.

At our house, we had a whole beautifully decorated guest room just sitting there—we only had overnight guests a couple of times a year. So it became my own private studio. The idea is to have some space where your stuff won't be disturbed, where you can feel creative and inspired. You can still wear your slippers, but whenever you are in your "space," you are all business.

* *Are you a good multitasker?* Can you wear many hats without getting too anxious or disorganized? Because while you will obviously spend a lot of time designing and making jewelry, you will spend more time running the business. Yes, you read that right—and you need it to sink in. You will spend more time doing the accounting, promotion, paperwork, selling, ordering, networking, and on and on than you will creating jewelry.

   Many times you will be doing several of these business-related things at once and you'll need not only to be able to keep your cool, but to embrace the process instead of letting it stress you out.

* *Do you have backup plans?* What will you do when you have rush orders or cash shortages, when you get sick right before an important show, when your kids are sick? Life happens, and you need contingency plans. We'll discuss the money part in later chapters, but the other issues just involve needing help.

My best advice: get a support system—one person or several people who are really on your team, who want to see you succeed. It's great if that can be your partner or spouse, but it's really helpful if it can also be fellow artists. It doesn't matter whether they are jewelry makers or not, you need people who are trying to sell their handmade art just like you, who understand what you're going through. Who will really get it when you don't get into a coveted show, or when you were shipped the wrong product after it had been backorder for six weeks, or when your town has had its first snowstorm of the year the weekend of your best show, or when the hottest boutique in town just placed its first order with you, or when you're being featured in a local magazine.

It's just so important to have someone who "gets" the business and can relate to what you're feeling during the highs and lows. I have a close group of bead store owner friends who make up my support system. I probably call or e-mail at least one of them every day, even though we all live in different parts of the country. They have saved my sanity countless times.

Defining your style of jewelry

If you put all your jewelry out on a table and had to describe its "look" or style, what words would come to mind? Contemporary? Art Deco? Vintage? Ethnic? Edgy? Playful? Being able to define your style verbally and in writing is one of the first steps in building your jewelry business.

It is a crucial step that will determine where your jewelry—and your business—go from here. Being able to clearly define your style, and by extension who your typical customer is, will help you keep a clear focus. Why? Because it's very difficult to sell a product if you don't know who you're selling it to. Your style will determine every decision you make about your business: the name, the logo, the promotional material you produce, the type of shows you do, the displays you create, the stores and galleries you approach. To use an extreme example, you wouldn't show your high-end semiprecious pieces at the flea market, because that's not the environment that attracts the customer you're trying to reach.

All successful designers have their own recognizable style. That is how they build a following—by having a very consistent look and identity. They attract people who become loyal, who check out their new collections each season, who seek them out at shows. Most women I know have a type of handbag they love or a certain brand of makeup or certain labels of clothing that fit them better than others. It's the same with their taste in handmade jewelry.

Let me give you an example. My friend Kate used to make one-of-a-kind multistrand necklaces that always had a tassel of beads as the focal point. Each necklace was different in pattern, color, and texture, but that tassel was always

Partying With the Wild-Haired Beaders

There's a group of women in my area who call themselves "the wild-haired beaders." They have been friends ever since their hippy biker chick days. They do jewelry in different media. They started doing holiday parties in one of their homes and eventually had to rent halls for their shows. The last one I went to was so well attended that I had to park blocks away. They recently disbanded because they had built their own individual followings—which was the purpose of the group from the beginning. It turned out to be a great experience from which everyone benefited.

Kate's necklaces are each one of a kind, but they share a signature beaded tassel. Courtesy of Kate Richbourg, Beadissimo, San Francisco, CA front and center. Eventually she stopped selling this design and started teaching it as a class at bead shows around the country. I would be at these shows and see ladies with their tassel necklaces and say to them, "Oh, you had a class with Kate?" And every time they would say "Yes—but how did you know?" How did I know? Because she had a distinctive style that I could recognize every time.

Even if you're just getting started in this business, if you've developed elements of style that people can recognize, you probably already have a following. Who are the people who always comment on the jewelry you wear every day? The folks at work who say, "You always have on the coolest jewelry?" The ones who often say, "I just love your designs?" I know this has happened to you a few times or you wouldn't be reading this book. The key is how to home in on your style and get it defined so you can make it work for you.

Here's another example. I know a designer in Dallas who makes very small rings in sterling silver and 14k gold. They're distinctly and consistently whimsical with stars, butterflies, fairies, and other charming motifs. But the rings aren't made for fingers! They're tiny and made to collect and hang off a cord or chain to be worn around the neck. This way her customers can keep buying more and more, unlike typical rings, for which you run out of fingers. People are excited to see her new collection each season. Her rings make great gifts because they fit everyone. She's used her marketing savvy to create a distinctive niche, and her company is doing millions of dollars a year in sales by focusing on that niche.

Think about creating a special niche for your jewelry that will not only set it apart, but will give you unique and targeted marketing opportunities. For instance:

* If you do a line of semiprecious stone jewelry and choose to market on the healing properties of the stones, then you could approach New Age shows or stores.
* If you do floral themes in seed beading or precious metal clay (PMC), you can approach florists or floral shows.
* If you focus on jewelry for men, you can market your work to hip men's boutiques.

I have one customer who makes pins of dogs. She decoupages a picture of the dog and then seed-beads around it. I don't have a dog, but apparently if you do, you want it on a pin, because she's doing gangbuster business. She's able to

Pam Phelps, La Femme Bijou

Pam's company, whose name means "the jewelry lady" in French, was born about seven years ago out of Pam's personal love of beads and jewelry. Pam tried many different ways of marketing her creations before coming up with a winning formula. She tried shows, home parties, and stores, all the while trying to create a line and marketing strategy that not only would sell well, but would work well with her life as a stay-at-home mom.

Her solution is to sell her jewelry at events in her home. Several times a year she sends out invitations, prepares a beautiful spread of food, and creates a lovely ambiance for a classy, intimate shopping experience. She also takes private appointments and special orders, all in her home, which keeps her expenses down, but also helps her keep that one-on-one connection with her customers.

That customer is typically a professional woman with disposable income who is looking for something different, so Pam creates unusual pieces that they wouldn't find in department stores. Her customers come back time and again, knowing Pam will have fresh new designs each season.

*Courtesy of
Pam Phelps,
La Femme Bijou,
Tacoma, WA*

Creating a customer profile

Here's a checklist of the kind of traits that will help you create a mental image of your typical customer. If you keep that image in your mind at all times, it will help you focus your business and build your brand. Create this imaginary person—you can even give her or him a name. Then when you come up with a new design, or when you're designing your portfolio, or when you're choosing a store or gallery to carry your work, you can ask yourself, "Would Pamela (or Tammy, or Gladys, or whoever) like this? Would she go there to shop?" It's a little mental game for helping you keep your focus.

* How old is she?
* Is she conservative or more free-spirited?
* How much money does she spend on herself?
* What's her style—traditional, punk, earthy, elegant?
* Is she a stay-at-home mom, or does she have an outside job?
* How often and how much does she dress up?
* What does she do for fun?
* Does she belong to clubs or other organizations?
* Where does she like to shop?
* Where does she go on vacation?
* And so forth.

market through such niche channels as pet shows and pet stores, and she has a special website where people can custom-order a pin featuring their dog and wear it proudly on their jacket

I'm sure you can think of dozens more examples. Just about every type of retail store these days has jewelry of some sort that complements its other merchandise: museums stores, gift stores, hair salons, the possibilities are endless. If your jewelry fits into a niche such as these, you'll have a nice edge in establishing repeatable sales.

If your jewelry falls into more of a mainstream, contemporary style instead of one of these specialty categories, don't despair. That may be the most saturated market, but it's also the largest and most affluent, and there's always room for something new.

Who is your customer? Who will buy your jewelry? You've got to be able to answer that question before you can take one more step. Is it teens, young women, mature women, men? The demographic of people who come into my store is women age thirty-five to sixty-five. If this is your customer, too, you've got a real challenge—it's definitely where you'll find the most competition. But there's still a place for you—you just have to get creative in how you think about your customer. In theory, she will have more money, her kids are older, she's more interested in nurturing herself with material goods, and best of all, there are more of her!

However, almost every woman I know loves "retail therapy," so if your designs are aimed at a younger crowd, say thirteen to twenty, or twenty to thirty-five, realize that and build from there. Everything you design from now on, from your jewelry, to your logo, to your show displays, will be aimed at enticing that customer now that you know who she is.

What if you still don't know? Here are a couple of simple exercises that will help you think about, test, and identify your personal style of work. If you're still looking at all your jewelry and you see some seed beading, some wirework, some PMC, some contemporary stringing—you really need to narrow your focus, because you're probably looking at four different customer types, at least. If you seriously want to start marketing and selling your work, you need to identify and stick with one style and build from there.

First, go from your soul.

* What style or medium really speaks to you?
* What really gets those creative juices flowing and what are you just dabbling in?
* Next, which styles are more marketable than others?
* Do any one of them have the kind of niche that we've discussed?

In the end, I believe that whatever you put your pure energy into will pay you back. That's just the way universe works.

Exercise I: Try selling at a local craft show. I mean the smallest show you can find, your church bazaar, your kid's school fair, or your town's local weekend market. We'll cover doing bigger shows later on. This type of show should be very inexpensive, $20 to $40 for a table or booth, so that you can at least make your fee back. Don't think of it as a money-making endeavor, though, but more as research. You need to really listen to folks, see which pieces they're commenting on, which they are ignoring. Many times the pieces that are not your personal favorites will be the most popular. Discovering what styles resonate with the public. Even if you end up going for a different, maybe more high-end demographic, this experience will help you immensely in thinking about your professional path and what type of jewelry you want to focus on.

Exercise II: Try having a home party. Many of my customers have tried them as an experiment and have had so much success that they've started doing them on a regular basis. You can have a party on your own, but I really think

Sample postcards for home jewelry parties. Courtesy of Jennifer Benoil, Firefly Jewelry Design, Tacoma, WA

it's more beneficial to invite other artists to join you. This is especially important in the beginning when your primary purpose is to get feedback and gain market knowledge.

Getting unbiased feedback is unlikely if the only people who attend are your friends and family. I would try to get at least three or four other artists —other jewelers or even quilters, card or candle makers, whatever would attract the same type of customer. Then all of you invite everyone you know. Ask on the invitation for that person to bring a friend in exchange for a free pair of earrings or a votive candle. The idea is to get as many people as possible to see your jewelry. Put out snacks, wine and cheese, nice music, candles, make an effort to put people in a buying mood. Then watch what they buy. You will learn a lot. If it does turn out to be financially successful for you, you could do it on a regular basis, with your friends or on your own eventually.

Nail it down. From what you know about yourself, and from getting your work out in front of the public for feedback, you should be able to narrow down and define your style. Having this information will help you in every step along your business journey. Here is an example of a fictitious jewelry business to show you some of the decisions that go into setting your course:

* *Jewelry style:* Contemporary large designs using only semiprecious stones.
* *Niche:* Focusing on the healing and positive energy from the stones to promote health as well as fashion to women forty to sixty-five years old.
* *Price point:* $50 to $1,000.
* *Name:* Gem's Wisdom.
* *Collateral materials:* Plum, burgundy, gold in muted matte tones, to use in business cards, hang tags, earrings cards, and background for promotional postcards. Matching fabric bags for each piece sold.

If you're still not there, don't be impatient with yourself but don't procrastinate, either. Go with what you have to get the process started. It is an absolute certainty that your style will evolve and you will be constantly updating your business as it grows and you grow into it.

Draw inspiration from the world around you. Really pay attention to what inspires you. At my store we keep an "inspiration book" for our customers, but also for us when we need some fresh ideas. We collect pictures of jewelry from catalogs, magazines, or websites and compile them in a notebook. We

Carrie Hamm,
Carrie Hamm Designs

Carrie started selling her designs about six years ago. Most of her customers, the shows she sells at, and the stores that carry her work are located in the Pacific Northwest, so she is very much in tune with what people in this region want.

Carrie's designs are earthy, clean, and simple, and they reflect the lifestyle of the thirty-something crowd. Keeping most of her price points in the mid range—earrings $18 to $30, bracelets and necklaces $24 to $100, also make them affordable for this age group.

Carrie advises new designers to find a way to set themselves apart in this competitive business and not to take rejections personally. She keeps good records of her show sales to track what's selling best, and she keeps her customer list updated so she can let them know when she has new designs or when she's appearing at an event.

Making and selling jewelry are part-time pursuits for Carrie—she has a full-time job (working for me at The Bead Factory!). She intends to continue focusing on the client base she has developed rather than growing it, so she can enjoy her jewelry making as a creative outlet that earns her extra income. This combination of a "day job" with creative, entrepreneurial sideline allows for a very healthy balance in her life.

Carrie Hamm
Designs

Locally Grown

Thank you for
supporting Tacoma
artists

Carrie Hamm
Designs

Carrie Hamm
Designs

$12.00

Carrie Hamm
Designs

Carrie Hamm
Designs

*Courtesy of Carrie
Hamm, Carrie Hamm
Designs, Tacoma, WA*

organize these by style, but you could do them by season or color or materials.

I receive hundreds of catalogs a month, and just about every one has jewelry that complements its primary product line. Many department stores, such as Nordstrom and Neiman Marcus, feature separate jewelry or accessories catalogs. If you're not receiving them now, just go to their websites and sign up. My favorite inspiration magazine by far is *InStyle*, because every month there's a six or eight-page section focusing specifically on whatever jewelry is popular right now. Plus this magazine features celebrities in Los Angles or New York. I don't know where you live, but here in Tacoma we are a good year behind whatever is hot, so for us (and most of the country) it's like a glimpse into the future. You'll find yourself inspired by color and material combinations, by striking clasps. Don't limit yourself to fashion magazines, though. Home décor and lifestyle magazines might have a beautiful flower arrangement on the cover—just the color palette to inspire a necklace.

Keeping it simple

One last word about developing your style. I have watched and known many jewelry designers over my twenty-plus years in this business; some of them succeed and some don't. Trust me—your designs absolutely do not have to be technically difficult to be successful. They don't even have to be especially original. In fact, the more labor intensive you make your work, the more you run the danger of pricing it out of the market.

I have seen many beadmakers fall into this trap. They might start doing dots or flowers, but pretty soon they're adding 14k gold leaf and several layers of casing and their beads, which sold at one time for $35, are suddenly $200 and not selling as well or attracting new audiences. There are precious few new ideas, so don't feel that you have to kill yourself trying to come up with one. Almost everything is just a variation of something else.

Don't overestimate your potential customer, either. You might go into a department store and see the simplest earrings on the rack for $45 and think "I could make that." Well, most people don't think that way. Most people want to buy their jewelry already made, and that's where you come in. A member of my staff makes the simplest little bracelets of fire-polished crystals, freshwater pearls, and pewter spacers. They sell for about $15 and come in every color you can imagine. At every show she participates in, she sells hundreds of dollars' worth of them. She could certainly do more elaborate or original work, but she's tuned into her market. She understands price point and quality and matches it to the customers she reaches through these shows.

Speaking of quality . . .

Let me touch for a moment on the quality of your jewelry. You'll really want to get any areas of uncertainty cleaned up before you put the jewelry out into the world. If there is a loop or crimp or some other technique that you're just not getting to perfection, please take a class, go to your local bead store, get a book, or e-mail me, and I'll point you in the right direction. Having quality jewelry will pay you back in the long run, but having poor-quality pieces can destroy your business before it even gets started. It's well worth the investment to put time and money in mastering proper techniques.

I'd also recommend you wear any new designs yourself for a few days to see how the piece lies around the neck or on the wrist and how comfortable it is, so you can make any changes before you take that design to market.

When I worked at Nordstrom in the jewelry department, we bought these huge earrings that were large pieces of crystal glued to a flat clip base that covered practically the entire ear (think 1980s). Every time we got a shipment from this designer, at least half had crystals broken from the base and had to be sent back. Worse than that, I was afraid to sell them to my customers because I knew they would just end up in the returns department. We eventually stopped buying from this particular designer and she went out of business. What a sad way to blow such a big account. Quality is something completely within your control, so take the time you need.

Two. Building Your Portfolio

For artists, a portfolio is a case for carrying their work. For artists in business, it's a collection of information and pictures about you and your work that you can take to potential customers of all kinds. It can be as simple as a folder that you keep adding to and updating. (But who knows? You might outgrow that format and need to get a professional catalog produced!)

Your portfolio will speak for you and your business to whomever you present it. This could be a retail store you are trying to sell your jewelry to, a juried craft show you are trying to get into, or a group gallery show that promises to give you good exposure.

What's in your portfolio?

Your portfolio should include:

* Artist biography
* Business card, postcard, or both
* A contact page with information about your business and how to get in touch with you
* At least one picture of your designs, though if you have several you should include whatever is appropriate for the recipient

The ultimate goal of the portfolio is to make a connection with the person you're approaching. I'll be talking about "making a connection" many times in these pages, and I'm not just talking abstractly. Because buying jewelry or art is about making a connection. No one needs jewelry, but people have adorned themselves since the beginning of time because it creates a feeling within them. Jewelry can make us feel special or beautiful or cherished or symbolize an important aspect of our lives—wedding rings and grandmother bracelets are cases in point. Or even those dog pins I described earlier. Most women I know have a need to set themselves apart with personal adornment, and jewelry is an important way of accomplishing that. As an artist, you must inspire a feeling of connection in the potential buyer. Your portfolio is a very important part of this process—creating that connection we're all looking for.

This all ties back into how you've defined your jewelry line and your market. Your portfolio should be an accurate reflection of your creative output, whether it's elegant, playful, practical, affordable, or luxurious. Did I say this before? I'll say it again. Be true to the style of your work. Vintage, modern, art deco, earthy . . . make sure everything you produce, every graphic design decision you make, is consistent with that style.

Creating promotional materials

After you have decided such basics as your jewelry style and the colors you'll use, it's time to put those all together in a package that reflects the image you're trying to create. This takes time, but it is creative time, and doesn't have to be expensive. Not having these materials is not an option in this day and age. It's a necessary investment, whether in the cost of your time and equipment or of paying someone else to do it for you. In decreasing order of cost (but increasing time investment), here are some ways to go about creating it.

Hire a professional. Keep an eye out for work you like—in other peoples' portfolios, in the local media—and find out who did it. Or visit the website of the American Institute of Graphic Arts (www.aiga.org) and check out portfolios of designers in your area. If you go this route, come to a clear understanding of what the scope of the work will be, what will become your property, and what it will cost.

Use student talent. Contact a local college or art school and ask to see the work of some of their top graphic design students. Maybe they'll do the work for you as part of a class project, or maybe they'll do it for a very reasonable fee so they'll have it to add to their own portfolio.

Do it yourself. There has never been a better time in the history of technology for creating nice-looking promotional materials on your own. You can create just about everything you need from a personal computer, printer, and digital camera. I'm going to give you some guidance in taking this route, because that's how I've done it and it's been both practical and rewarding. Here we go.

Choosing a name

This is a key first step in creating your brand. Many people just use their own name, especially if they're doing one-of-a-kind work. Whether that's your choice or not, do consider including some jewelry-related term in the title. Jewelry, custom jewelry, beadwork, baubles, bling. It will get across what kind of business yours is and will help people find you. But think about the impression your business name will make on potential customers. There's a world of difference between Barbie's Baubles and Barbara Norton Custom Jewelry. They both work—but for different markets, different styles.

Type style

Next, how to present that name—what type style, what kind of logo, if any. Look at the name in many different type styles. Look at it with and without some sort of logo or symbol. It's not a make-or-break element, but it's fun to have a logo to stamp on metal hang tags or on the bags you put the jewelry in when you sell it. Just make sure it matches your style and is not too complicated with too many colors or special graphic effects. Too many of these and you'll run into problems when printing bags, boxes, pens, and so forth.

Paper

Even if you've had someone else do the design work, you'll probably be printing a lot of your promotional materials yourself, using your own color printer. Paper choices should fit aesthetically with the total package. I recommend white glossy photo paper for pictures of your work (you can buy it at any office supply or discount store), and definitely basic white paper for miscellaneous information—Regular 20# bond will do.

But then have some fun exploring different kinds of paper to find just the right one for your bio/contact sheets, price lists, hang tags and earrings cards. Shops that carry rubber stamping products have a large selection of styles, weights, and colors to choose from. You'll find corrugated papers, suede papers, and handmade papers. Some are made to print on, some you can just use for

My friend Jennifer makes very large, organic wirework jewelry, very modern with really fun colors and shapes. Her company's name is Kiss of Life; her logo is a round scroll with a square one on either side of the name. The font—that's the alphabet style—is playful and energetic. For pieces she prints herself, such as hang tags and price lists, she cuts the edges of the paper a little wonky to match the look of her jewelry. All of her promotional materials, from logo to earrings cards, convey the same sense of fun as her jewelry. And ultimately, the fact that she "has it together" will result in more orders. Besides giving her customers confidence with her consistency and professionalism, it makes Jennifer herself feel more confident in her business because she has invested time in clearly defining her business and its presentation. You can do the same.

Courtesy of Jennifer Ratajik, Kiss of Life, Seattle, WA

backgrounds or display. Choose a cardstock weight for earrings cards and hang tags or for business cards if you're printing your own.

So now you've got the name, fonts, paper . . . let's get to work putting it together. Even if someone is doing it for you, you have to be very active in the design process because they have to get all the necessary information from you, and you have to give a lot of input on how it looks.

Contact page

The first page of your portfolio should include your biography, perhaps a picture of you and/or your studio, and all the necessary contact information: address, phone numbers, e-mail address, website. It might also have your ordering policies or product information. Also somewhere on your contact sheet if there's room, you might want to add comments other customers have made to you about your jewelry. These are called testimonials and they are free! Just ask the person who said it to you if you can quote them in your promotional material. People love to see their names in print.

Writing your artist's biography

Writing about yourself in a professional context can be pretty intimidating. Just bear in mind that you're just writing a short story about you, how you got started, what inspires you now, some personal information such as where you live and if you're married or have kids, and so forth.

The goal here is to make that connection. The more someone knows about you, the artist, the more connected that person feels to you, and the more comfortable they will feel doing business with you. Look at other artists' biographies online to get some ideas. If you're really not comfortable writing about yourself, ask someone to write it for you. Keep it simple: write down much more information than you need and than just edit it down to some key points. Normally it's not much longer than four or five sentences, such as:

> *Andrea's Adornments*
> Andrea Gibson has been creating jewelry for four years. She has a background in graphic design and photography. Her jewelry designs of stones and pearls are inspired by the natural beauty in the forests around her home near Ashland, Oregon. Andrea divides her time between making jewelry, doing craft shows, and chasing after of her three-year-old daughter, Michelle.

A lifetime passion for jewelry, color, and design has evol

Distant Lands — jewelry by design

Since 1999 we've created distinctive designs by blending b together from around the world: Italy, Japan, India, the UK, Indonesia, Thailand, the US, and more. Republic, the UK, Indonesia, Thailand, the US, and more. The beads are made of various materials, primarily glass treate many ways, as well as various agates, jaspers, porcelain, semi-precious stones, lustrous pearls and more.

Some of our suppliers create beautiful handmade glass beads using a torch and glass canes in various colors. From others we find carved bone and stone pendants to use as stunning focal pieces for unique necklaces with an exotic look.

The creative spirit behind the company is Valerie Oliver, a Northwest artist living in Tacoma, Washington. Valerie's travels around the world have given her an appreciation for many forms of art and jewelry. She searches out unique and interesting components, and looks to the beauty in life as inspiration for her evolving designs.

Much of our jewelry is either one-of-a-kind pieces or limited editions. Please contact us if you have a specific idea in mind, we may have exactly what you desire.

❖ Custom orders are welcome ❖

Thank you for choosing this piece of *Distant Lands Jewelry.*
We hope you thoroughly enjoy your wearable art!

Valerie Oliver, designer & proprietor
Tacoma, Washington USA
phone: 253-279-0310
e-mail: DistantLands@mindspring.com

Courtesy of Valerie Oliver,
Distant Lands Jewelry,
Tacoma, WA

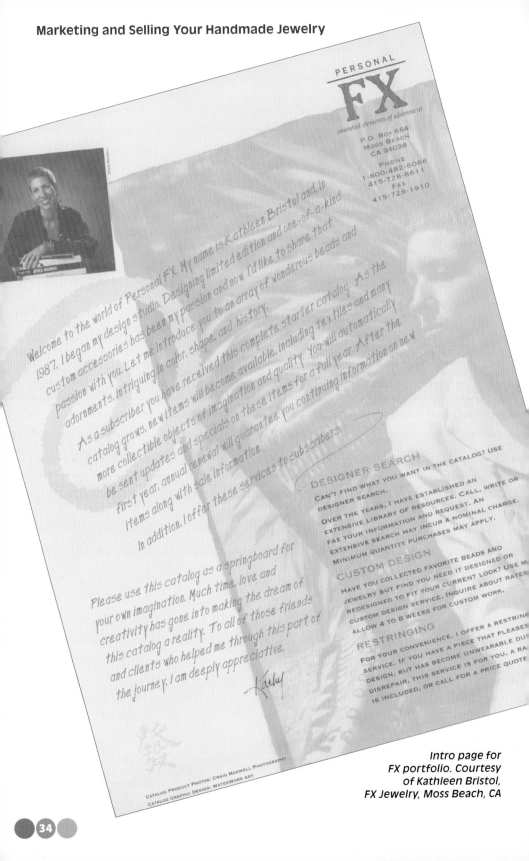

PERSONAL

FX

essential elements of adornment

P.O. Box 664
MOSS BEACH
CA 94038

PHONE
1-800-482-6066
415-728-8611
FAX
415-728-1910

Welcome to the world of Personal FX. My name is Kathleen Bristol and, in 1987, I began my design studio. Designing limited edition and one-of-a-kind custom accessories has been my passion and now I'd like to share that passion with you. Let me introduce you to an array of wonderous beads and adornments, intriguing in color, shape, and history.

As a subscriber you have received this complete starter catalog. As the catalog grows, new items will become available, including textiles and many more collectible objects of imagination and quality. You will automatically be sent updates and specials on these items for a full year. After the first year, annual renewal will guarantee you continuing information on new items along with sale information.

In addition, I offer these services to subscribers:

Please use this catalog as a springboard for your own imagination. Much time, love and creativity has gone into making the dream of this catalog a reality. To all of those friends and clients who helped me through this part of the journey, I am deeply appreciative.

Kathy

DESIGNER SEARCH

CAN'T FIND WHAT YOU WANT IN THE CATALOG? USE DESIGNER SEARCH.

OVER THE YEARS, I HAVE ESTABLISHED AN EXTENSIVE LIBRARY OF RESOURCES. CALL, WRITE OR FAX YOUR INFORMATION AND REQUEST. AN EXTENSIVE SEARCH MAY INCUR A NOMINAL CHARGE. MINIMUM QUANTITY PURCHASES MAY APPLY.

CUSTOM DESIGN

HAVE YOU COLLECTED FAVORITE BEADS AND JEWELRY BUT FIND YOU NEED IT DESIGNED OR REDESIGNED TO FIT YOUR CURRENT LOOK? USE M CUSTOM DESIGN SERVICE. INQUIRE ABOUT RATES ALLOW 4 TO 8 WEEKS FOR CUSTOM WORK.

RESTRINGING

FOR YOUR CONVENIENCE, I OFFER A RESTRING SERVICE. IF YOU HAVE A PIECE THAT PLEASES DESIGN, BUT HAS BECOME UNWEARABLE DU DISREPAIR, THIS SERVICE IS FOR YOU. A RA IS INCLUDED, OR CALL FOR A PRICE QUOTE

CATALOG PRODUCT PHOTOS: CRAIG MAXWELL PHOTOGRAPHY
CATALOG GRAPHIC DESIGN: WATERWORK ART

Intro page for
FX portfolio. Courtesy
of Kathleen Bristol,
FX Jewelry, Moss Beach, CA

Photographs of your work

Perhaps the biggest element in your portfolio will be product shots—the photographs of your designs. Do them yourself or hire someone to do them—but having them is not optional. Doing them yourself, if you're properly equipped, will give you a lot of freedom to change your promotional materials as you need to, which could be quite often. It will also save you a lot of money in the long run. With all the digital equipment with automatic features out there today, just about anyone can become a decent enough photographer. You'll find your photos don't always have to be professional quality to work. As long as they show your work, are in focus, and well lit, and as long as people can tell what they're looking at, they'll be good enough for many purposes.

So how will you use these great pictures? Make your own business cards. Create pages for your portfolio. Document your inventory of finished work (keep it in your computer or make a book that customers can browse through). But one of the most productive uses of a good product shot is to produce a postcard.

What you'll need for great pictures

To do it all yourself you'll definitely be investing some money and some time to learn how to get those great pictures. But it will be one of the best investments you'll ever make because you'll have a lot of control and flexibility, and you'll save money in the long run. The basics outlined below will add up to about $1,000.

* Camera. I thoroughly believe that you get what you pay for, so don't go for cheap on this. At the same time, you don't need top-of-the line. A digital camera that will take care of most or all of your needs will probably be in the $300 range as of this writing.
* Lights. We bought two very bright lamps at a local camera store just for the kind of still shots we planned to do.
* Hardware. You'll need a computer and color printer.
* Software. You'll need some image-editing software such as Photoshop. This will allow you to take out shadow lines, alter the color, even erase mistakes or dings in your wirework that you may not have noticed.
* Photo box or light box to help you keep lighting uniform and under control.

Take a class, get a little consulting time with a professional photographer, or have a pro from your local camera shop help you set up and master the basics.

The 10th Annual

Puget Sound

Bead Festival!

July 15th, 16th & 17th, 2005
Friday & Saturday 10-6 Sunday 11-5

Tacoma Sheraton Convention Center
1320 Broadway Ave., Tacoma, WA

Featuring 100 booths!
Over 60 classes!

Call (253) 572-5529 or
1-888-500-BEAD for more info
or a show program.
$6 Admission – good for both days
www.PugetSoundBeadFestival.com

*Full color postcards don't have to be
expensive. Courtesy of The Bead
Factory, Inc., Tacoma, WA*

Postcards

There are companies that specialize in printing full-color postcards for as little as $100 for 500 cards. It's a quick process—you can e-mail one of your images and a text file of the information you want on the reverse side (contact information, maybe a brief description of the piece shown on the front). You'll have your cards within three weeks. I've used Modern Postcard in Carlsbad, California (www.modernpostcard.com), and you'll find others online that offer similar services.

With your contact information on the back of your postcard, you can use it as a business card, have a stash handy to give people who ask about your work when you're wearing it, provide a stack for the taking when you're doing shows, leave some at galleries or boutiques that carry your work.

If you sell at a lot of shows, you can put your show schedule on the reverse of your postcard and mail it your customer list. A lot of people collect them—it's hard to lose or throw away a handsome color postcard!

You can also use postcard printers to create full-color business cards (facing page). Instead of having one image on the front, have four of the same (or four different ones) printed on each card. Have your contact information printed four times on the reverse. Cut them up, and voila! You have 2,000 really striking business cards for just $100! That's incredibly cheap and much more effective than a business card that just says "Jenny's Jewels."

Portfolio pages

If your designs are all one of a kind, the pictures in your portfolio only need to be representative of what you have on hand. This is the kind of portfolio you would produce to approach galleries or jurors for higher-

Don't get caught up in ego

It's very easy to lose sight of what you're trying to accomplish when you're in the process of designing your promotional pieces. Some designers (I'm often guilty myself) put so much emphasis on looking "cool" that the details of their work don't show well. This kind of presentation can look edgy and fresh, but it loses its purpose—which is to inspire someone to buy something or place an order. So before you put something out there, please stop and put yourself in the customer's place. Better still, ask some friends or family members—ones who will give you honest opinions—to give your promotional material a trial run.

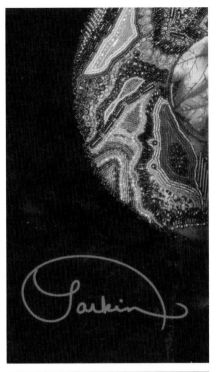

Online postcard printing companies make it possible to print business cards with several full-color designs on one side, and black-and-white information on the back. Courtesy of Larkin Jean Van Horn, Freeland, WA

Larkin Jean Van Horn

Art Quilts

Wearable Art

Beadwork

P.O. Box 1478

Freeland, WA 98249

Fax: (360) 341-4360

Phone: (360) 341-4377

larkin@larkinart.com

http://www.larkinart.com

end craft shows. But if you're doing limited production runs, you'll need a more of a buyer-friendly catalog format, with product codes and available colors. This kind of portfolio usually shows several pieces on a page.

One clever format I've seen is an 8½ by 11 inch page of photographic paper divided horizontally into thirds. Each third has a picture with the description next to it. These pages can be cut into thirds, mixed and matched, and fit into a standard number 10 envelope in an attractive color. This allows a lot of flexibility—pieces can be added or deleted and matched to the needs of a particular buyer or gallery owner.

Beautiful portfolio photography can be a showstopper. Courtesy of Kathleen Bristol, FX Jewelry, Moss Beach, CA

A well-planned portfolio.
Courtesy of Kathleen Bristol, FX Jewelry, Moss Beach, CA

Price sheet

In addition to your contact sheet, bio, and pictures, you need a price sheet. You might need two—one wholesale and one retail, which we'll discuss later. But you'll want the price sheet to be a separate piece. Don't *ever* print prices on the pictures, or you won't have the flexibility to change them. If material costs go up, or some other variable changes that makes it impossible to produce a piece for the price you originally put on it, it's easier and cheaper to adjust a price list than to redo picture pages.

The package

Now that you have everything together, you'll want to find a nice folder to put it all into. You can put a label printed with your logo on the outside, cut the edges in some unique way, use rubber stamps—something to make your portfolio stand out among others. Avoid odd sizes—think about what will be easy and inexpensive to mail.

You have a lot of options when designing your portfolio. You can start simple and upgrade as your career grows. Just remember that your portfolio is the first impression you'll be making for many galleries or show organizers, and first impressions go a long way.

Display materials

If you plan to sell at a show, you'll need a whole different kind of promotional material: earrings cards, hang tags for necklaces or bracelets, bags for the pieces you sell, and signs or props for your table or booth. You

Earrings cards and tags with consistent design.
Courtesy of Christine Lutschg, Christine's Designs, Tacoma, WA

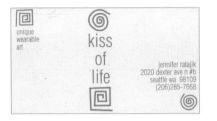

unique
wearable
art

kiss
of
life

jennifer ratajik
2020 dexter ave n #b
seattle wa 98109
(206)285-7668

beads.hammered.sterling

shown in first catalog photo. hammered sterling silver geometrical shapes mixed
with czech glass beads. these were my first designs and continue to be
important staples.
small earrings.10.00 (a106) bigger earrings.13.00 (a101) bracelet.18.00 (a102)
choker.23.00 (a103)20".26.00 (a107) 24".29.00 (a108) 28".32.00 (a109) 32".35.00 (a110)
36".38.00 (a104) 40".41.00 (a105) abstract hoop 12.00(a113) wrapped bead 9.00 (f601s)

hammered.sterling

shown in second catalog photo. hammered sterling silver geometrical shapes
connectedto form a very fluid design. looks great paired with other
beaded pieces!
small earrings.11.00 (b208) bigger earrings.13.00 (b201) bracelet.18.00 (b202)
choker.27.00 (b20?) ?9.00 (b209) 24".33.00 (b210) 28".37.00 (b211)
32"._ (b204) 40".49.00 (b205) hoop earring.13.00 (d401) (please

_oto. in this line i've used hammered blackened steel
_ed czech glass beads. this creates a very dramatic
selling lines.
_gger earrings.13.00(c301) bracelet.18.00 (c302)
_rop.32.00 (c304) 20".34.00 (c309) 24".38.00 (c310)
_) 36".47.00 (c305) 36" with drop.50.00 (c306)
_7.00 (f601)

_mi-precious stones joined with shiny sterling
_refined and delicate than some of my other
_ng pieces.
_ed earring.9.00 (g712) bigger earrings.
_hoker.25.00(g704) 17" with drop.27.00(g705)
_.35.00 (g710) 32".38.00 (g711) 36".41.00 (g706)

_glass beads creates a bold heavy chain.
_with the other steel lines! add SS

_ium bead earring 8.00 (i91?'
_(i901) large earring'
_charm brace'
_00 (i91?'

a101
b201
b208
c301
a106
g702s
j1002
c308
d401
g701s

more earrings

necklace & bracelet patterns

Kiss of Life materials.
Courtesy of Jennifer Ratajik,
Kiss of Life, Seattle, WA

really need to get this all together before you start pricing you pieces, so that you can figure these expenses in to the equation. The possibilities are endless, but keep in mind that your packaging and signage need to be appropriate to the kind of work you do and consistent with the design or your portfolio.

Spend some time on this. Take a trip to the fabric store, look at ribbons and cloth, go to the rubber stamp store, look at papers and deckle scissors. Look at other shows or in other stores, see what other artists have done. Packaging is an important part of what makes a product sell, and besides that, it's fun!

Try different approaches. Do you want your earrings to be attached to cards, lie in boxes, hang from a rack, or lie in a tray? Never buy the generic earrings cards. It's so easy to make your own and to enhance your image in the process. Will you use a hang tag with your necklaces? What will you tie it on with? Ribbon, wire, silk? Will you print the cards or hand-stamp them? Will you include just your name and logo or add a description of the piece?

One jewelry maker I know specializes in high-end pieces, in the range of $300 for a necklace. She names each one of her necklaces and uses it on the hang tag: Jessica, Marie, real names with a description of what stones and other materials are in the piece. It doesn't cost a thing to create this special little aura around each piece, and I promise you if two necklaces are lying side by side in a case, everything else being fairly equal, the one with the name will sell first. Why? Because it makes that connection with the customer, it feels more personal, and—did I say this before? Selling jewelry is about making a connection.

prices

beads.hammered.sterling
earrings.28.00 bracelet 32.00 choker.40.00 36".56.00 40".64.00

hammered.sterling
earrings.26.00 bracelet.30.00 choker.50.00 36".80.00 40".90.00
single ring.24.00 double ring.26.00 bangle.32.00

beads.steel
earrings.28.00 bracelet.32.00 choker.50.00 17" with drop.60.00
36".90.00 36" with drop.100.00 40".100.00

etc.
hair stix.20.00.pair hair pins.12.00.pair napkin rings.6.00.each
$ clip.10.00

Kiss of Life earrings card and price list. Courtesy of Jennifer Ratajik, Kiss of Life, Seattle, WA

Three. Pricing Your Work

It may seem backward to put development of promotional materials ahead of pricing, but in fact, the cost of those materials have to be figured into the price of your pieces. Neglecting to account for those costs is a common mistake of beginners in business, and it can make the difference between a profit and no profit.

Pricing is by far the most challenging part of this business for new designers. You want to make a profit, but you might not feel confident in the worth of your work yet. It's common for newbies in the world of commerce to underprice their work because they're afraid it won't sell otherwise. In other words, they make emotional decisions about pricing, which is really a numbers game.

If pricing is a hang-up for you, I'll show you how to play the two-step game of figuring out the proper pricing for your work and then marketing it so it will sell at the price it needs to be.

The perils of pricing too low

People generally do *not* buy jewelry based on price—they're not buying produce, after all—they buy it based on how they feel. Their jewelry-buying is based on emotion and connection. Women do sometimes need to justify their purchases, and that's where you need to be prepared to educate your customer on the value of what she's buying.

If you price your work very low, you are starting a losing battle. You can't compete with jewelry made overseas, and why would you want to? Don't fall into the trap of running your own personal sweatshop. Look at your handmade jewelry more as art than craft, and you will understand and appreciate its value more readily.

In my opinion, American artists can be successful only in the mid- to upper-price ranges, with an emphasis on the latter. Don't even think of putting your work in the same category as imported jewelry. Once you apply my formula to your jewelry and get the correct pricing, I think you will understand why contemporary jewelry is so expensive. If after doing these exercises you think, "I can't charge that for my jewelry, no one will buy it!" my response is, if you don't believe in yourself and your work, no one else will, either. Or in the great words of Zig Ziglar, "Whether you believe that you can, or believe that you can't, you're probably right."

Big decision: wholesale or retail?

If you *ever* plan to sell your jewelry to a store or a gallery or a catalog retailer, you will need to have a wholesale price, and that wholesale price will drive all your other pricing decision. The wholesale price is the lowest amount you'll ever sell your work for, and it simply has to include all your costs and a profit.

Generally speaking, the retail price—what your piece will cost the individual who ultimately buys it—is just double the wholesale price (also known as the "keystone"). For example, if a store buys your earrings for $20, they will probably sell them for around $40. All major department store chains work this way. Smaller boutiques may add a little more to cover more of their overhead. Galleries may not mark up this much if your work is in the mid-price range because they generally have much higher end-pieces that cover more of their overhead.

So unless you don't expect to ever sell except direct to individuals, your first step in the pricing game is to figure out your wholesale price. Then if you're selling at a craft fair or a retail jewelry show (one open to the public), or even just selling to the friend of a friend, you can just double that wholesale price to get your retail price.

I would encourage you to be consistent and not be lured into marking your prices at wholesale when you're doing a retail show, for several reasons. First, while double the wholesale price might seem like a big mark-up, the truth is that every day you're at a show is a day you are not at home making jewelry, and you need to be compensated for that time. Second, many shop owners frequent local shows to find new artists and just keep in touch with what's out there. If a shop owner inquires about your jewelry, she may ask if you have a wholesale discount. You can say yes, it is keystone, or half of the marked price (with a certain dollar minimum, which we'll talk about next).

Setting minimums for wholesale orders

Only you can decide what dollar minimum will make it worthwhile to sell at wholesale discounts. It can be $100, $250, $500—it's up to you, but most people start small and increase it as they gain experience. Say you are selling your work at a craft show, and you're approached by a retail boutique owner. You might say that your minimum is $150, meaning she'll select $300 worth of product at its full retail price, and it will cost her $150, or keystone. It's also up to you whether you want her to take your stock on the spot or set up an appointment so she can place an order later. I would suggest the latter because if she takes items from your show stock, you'll have nothing left to sell at full retail. Of course, if you have plenty of stock, or it's the last day of the show, or it's going slowly, it might be to your advantage to make the sale right then.

Enforcing the minimum is important, though. Do not be lured into, "I just want to try a few pairs for my shop, and then if they sell well, I'll order more." This is code for, "I just want to buy some for myself and my mom and I don't want to pay full price." Any professional store buyer respects and adheres to minimums to buy wholesale. A business license is not a license to buy everything half price. It's a license that allows a legitimate retail store owner to buy at volume discounts so they can make money when they resell the work.

Maybe most important, though, is that if you do sell to a shop owner in your area and then turn around and sell at the local Saturday market for less than she has it marked in her store, she'll probably stop buying from you and you'll lose that account. And she *will* find out. People talk. So don't undercut your own wholesale accounts. It's not professional, and you'll only be hurting yourself in the long run.

Calculating wholesale price

Four expenses go into the wholesale price of jewelry.

Materials. This is the actual cost of the materials in any given design. Every bead, every inch of wire, every bit of glue, yes, even seed beads—they weren't free last time I checked. You have to count everything. Ideally you'll record the cost of each product when you buy it. So if you buy a strand of pearls, calculate the cost per pearl as soon as you can and then label it with the cost per each. Do the same with chain or wire, cost per inch or foot depending on how you use it. Remember to figure in shipping if applicable.

Labor. Time is money, all right, and the cost of your labor is the time you spend designing and making your jewelry—but that's not all. As I mentioned earlier, making jewelry is not what's going to take the most of your time. You'll be doing sales and marketing and bookkeeping and portfolio work and sitting at shows and meeting with customers and so forth.

Unless your jewelry-making is a full-time, 9-to-5 job, you need to keep careful track of the time you do spend on the business. I recommend you get a small notebook to keep in your handbag or glove box or keep track on your electronic PDA. Every time you do any work, just jot down how much time it was and on what. This will definitely include design and production time, but also make sure to include shopping for materials, doing price comparisons, ordering materials, making phone calls of all kinds, travel, price calculating, design and production time on promotional materials, creating price lists, doing photography, doing paperwork, bills, taxes, show applications . . . just to name a few!

So every time you're driving home from your "day job" and decide to pop into the bead store for some crimp tubes (and before you know it, it's an hour later) or you're just going to check out a website you heard about and before you know it, you've spent three hours online, write it all down. You will be astonished at the amount of time all of this takes. After several months, you'll be able to go back and see how many hours a month you're spending on all these miscellaneous tasks. Make tracking your time a permanent habit.

Overhead. These are fixed expenses that for a lot of businesses are the same each month—rent, insurance, and so forth. If you're working at home, your business overhead expenses will vary from month to month, but would include: office supplies, show fees, equipment of all kinds—jewelry tools, fax machine, camera—also display materials, travel expenses, and always a few more you haven't counted on. The easiest way to track overhead expenses is with a separate checking account and/or a credit card. Then after three to six months, take all the expenses you've incurred and divide it by however many months it's been.

For example, say you've spent $3,600 over six months, which averages

$600 monthly overhead. If you produced 100 pieces in a given month, you would divide $600 by 100 pieces, which equals $6 of overhead for each piece.

Profit. Profit is what you need to stay in business—it is *not* what you pay yourself. That amount is figured into labor. Profit is what you make after you've paid all your expenses, including yourself. It would be great if the profit was just cash that piled up in the bank account—however, that is not what happens. What *does* happen is you'll use that profit to continually reinvest in your business. Profit allows you to buy that new camera or software, get larger quantities of inventory, do more promotional pieces—whatever it is that will help keep your business growing. I still reinvest every penny back into my business, because I continually see opportunities for growth. That, or I just never run out of ways to spend money. Either way, it's important to keep that profit coming.

How much do I pay myself?

It all boils down to one main question—how much money are you going to make doing this? We make jewelry for the love of jewelry, but all the love in the world won't pay the bills. Some people get very weird when it comes to speaking of money in exact dollar amounts. I am not one of those people. You can make a lot of money in this business. The opportunity is completely unlimited, and it depends totally on how much effort you're willing to put into your business.

Most jewelry designers I know try to allow themselves a starting pay rate of around $20 an hour, with the idea that they can give themselves a bonus whenever the business allows it. But once you begin working for yourself, days of regular paychecks are over. The newly self-employed pay themselves when they can and usually only when they need it to pay their personal bills. Most people who are serious about creating a future keep every penny that they can in the business. That being said, here's a fictitious story that might help you in costing your jewelry.

The pricing formula

Jo Ann Jewelry Designer has just quit her full-time job to work on her jewelry career, so we're going to start with her current salary. I've rounded a lot of the numbers for ease of calculation. Jo Ann has done her time logs and knows her overhead expenses. She used to make $14 an hour at her eight-hour-a-day job, or a total of $112 dollars a day. We'll round that down to $100.

It takes her about two hours a day to do the various business-management-related tasks, which leaves her six hours a day to produce jewelry. In those six hours, let's say she has made twenty pairs of earrings. Assuming $100 is her desired daily salary, she would divide this by the number of pairs produced to get the labor part of her equation: $100 divided by 20 = $5 per pair. Another way to say it: desired salary divided by units produced equals your labor cost per unit. So here's how Jo Ann would figure costs for a pair of her earrings:

Materials $3 (small pearls, a few crystals, simple)
+ Labor $5 (from calculation above)
= Total $8

At this point, Jo Ann doesn't have an exact idea of her overhead or desired profit, so to be on the safe side, she will double her materials and labor cost to get a wholesale cost, or keystone, of $16. She would double that again to arrive at the correct retail price of $32.

To summarize:

Materials and labor $8
+ Overhead $4
+ Profit $4
= Wholesale $16
Double that again to sell at retail at $32

Because you can calculate the materials and labor cost exactly, it's reasonable to double them to get a ballpark amount to cover overhead and profit. And I believe it's better to err on the high side because there are always so many forgotten expenses and endless amounts of time that we forget to track into our calculation.

This can all seem overwhelming at first. It will get easier. What I've given you is a general pricing guide for the craft industry, and you can adjust it to fit your business. You might find, for instance, if you use this formula on an elaborate multistrand necklace, it would end up being hundreds of dollars, more than your market will bear. Maybe you'd do a lower mark-up on the necklace and make it up in simpler earrings or bracelets.

Pricing is a big challenge for everyone in the beginning. You may go through several formulas to find the right one for you so be patient. You'll find little tricks to stretch your dollars. You'll find less expensive beads that work just fine for some designs. You'll just get smarter in general about how this all works.

One last note. I've noticed that a lot of people include sales tax in their price instead of charging it separately. I would discourage you from doing this. First, sales tax rates are different everywhere you sell. Plus, people already expect to pay sales tax, so don't make your jewelry appear more expensive than it actually is. If you put the sales tax in the price, you'll find a lot of confusion when it comes time to make your tax payments. Pricing is already enough work—give yourself a break.

Let your computer do it. There's a great software program called Jewelry Designer Manager (see Resource List on page 94). It keeps track of your entire loose inventory and components and also tracks finished pieces using photographs you attach to the file. You enter the markup percentages you want to use for each type of jewelry or buyer. For example, one page might include a picture of one of your necklaces, the cost of materials, and the different mark-ups you have set for wholesale and retail. It pays for itself quickly in just the time it saves.

Jewelry Design Manager also has an in-between price called "direct." I call this your "friends and family" discount, and it's very helpful for avoiding tricky situations as you grow. If you set up a direct discount that seems fair from the beginning, then you can just say, "I give 20 percent (or whatever) off for friends and family." But don't offer wholesale to this special category of customer— that is *not* fair to you. You should set this policy whether you're using software to calculate pricing or not.

Reality check

Let's say you've done these calculations and your prices are still coming up too high. Not too high based on your feeling about the value of your work but too high based on what's out there in department stores, catalogs, and from other artists. In other words, the real world. There are a couple things you can do to get prices down. The first, and this will happen automatically, you will get faster. That's been the experience of every jewelry designer I've known. You'll get faster at making your pieces, faster at producing promotional material, faster at ordering. So your labor cost in each piece will drop. The second, buy your materials for less.

Buying wholesale

Everyone wants to be able to buy their materials for less. To do so, you have to become a detective, not just in price comparison, but more importantly, in recognizing the quality of the product. There are a lot of different qualities of garnets, freshwater pearls, crystals, glass beads, and on and on. So first, you must first get educated on what you're buying and then decide which pieces *must* use sterling silver and which designs are just fine with pewter.

How much of a difference will it make in the final piece if the crystals are from China or Austria? Or if the pearls are real or very good fakes? Only you can decide. Obviously everyone likes the high-quality material, but you must take cost into consideration. So before you start shopping around, get very clear on what you need.

There's a lot of information out there. Go online, talk to your local bead shop owner, talk to wholesale representatives at bead shows, read the magazines and books. I actually teach a whole class just on how to buy beads. But in general, you get what you pay for. If you've found stones at an unbelievable price, then they are probably not real. Build relationships with vendors and buy from them consistently so you can trust the quality of the product. Plus the more you do business with someone, the better deals they are likely to give you.

Get a business license. The first step for buying wholesale is obtaining a business license. Do not attempt to use your husband's plumbing business license just because you don't want to do the paperwork, or you want to fly under the radar. We'll talk about licenses in future chapters. But you have no right to buy wholesale until you've obtained the proper license.

License in hand, attend your local bead and gem shows—every major city has at least one. What's nice about shows is that you can meet vendors face to face and see their products. I would discourage you from buying beads online until you've established a face-to-face relationship with the company. With materials such as pearls or stones, judging quality is completely based on feeling the weight and seeing the surface of the beads. All computer monitors are different, so it's almost impossible to really judge by online pictures.

And at shows, you can not only compare qualities and prices, but also pay attention to how you're treated. You'll want to start a relationship with someone who treats you well and appreciates your business. Do not reward bad service by spending your money there. There are hundreds of suppliers, and you'll always be able to find what you need somewhere else.

Develop vendor relationships. Most vendors don't post their wholesale prices or policies at shows, so you'll have to ask. Many are also leery of ques-

Tucson!

I can't mention vendors without saying that you must get yourself to Tucson during the first two weeks of February each year. The entire bead universe gathers there. It is not very expensive to go, but if you don't book your hotel months in advance you may not find a place to stay. There are at least twenty bead shows going on all over the city with shuttle buses between each one. This is by far the best bead shopping on the planet, and the perfect place to find new suppliers. Don't go with less than $1,000 to spend, and plan on staying at least three days, because you will never get these deals again. It's a nice change of weather toward the end of winter and a great place to connect with other people in the business.

tions because there are so many people trying to buy beads cheaper for their personal use. Be professional; tell the merchant up front you are a designer and ask "what is your wholesale policy?" instead of "what are your wholesale prices?" Just this little turn of phrase will make all the difference in how you are treated and possibly in what prices you'll be quoted.

Asking about the policy will tell you the dollar amount you need to spend (there's usually a minimum) and what the discount will be. You can ask if there are further discounts with larger quantities. I understand the need to get the smallest amount possible when you are starting out, but if your cash flow allows you to take advantage of larger discounts, you'll see a huge impact on your bottom line. It may only be a 2 percent discount here or 5 percent for cash, but it all adds up. I would recommend that you buy the largest quantity you can, within reason. Some things, jump rings for instance, are sold by the kilo (that's over two pounds!). If a kilo is a lifetime supply (unless you're doing chain mail), then maybe getting that big discount is *not* the best use of your cash.

Over time you will develop good, solid relationships with your vendors; they will become priceless as you grow. There will be time when you need a special favor, like a rush order or a check held for a couple weeks. You will only get these types of favors by building your bead family of suppliers.

Four. Selling Your Jewelry at Craft Shows

Believe it or not, only now are you ready to sell your work. Everything up to this point has been the prep work. Now let's go through some of the many different options and avenues for selling your work.

Regardless of whether your ultimate goal is to have a catalog, sales reps, your own gallery, or be a private stylist to movie stars—I think everyone needs to start with doing some craft shows. Why? Because shows will prepare you for any other direction you decide to go. They give you exposure and experience with the public, they let you try new designs and pricing structures, and they give you the chance to network with other people in the same business.

The lessons and experience you gain from doing shows is priceless, but shows can also be very profitable. They allow you exposure so you can build a following and a mailing list. Gaining and maintaining a loyal customer base is like money in the bank because repeat business is much easier to get than new business.

Artists don't generally do big advertising campaigns; their business tends to be built on word of mouth. As soon as you develop a small clientele, they will start bringing more and more people to see you, and pretty soon you've got a following. You might start by doing a lot of shows each year, but as time goes by you'll find the ones that attract the right kind of customer for your work. You just have to find the right shows and then maximize your potential at them.

Finding a show

I hear many horror stories from artists who have done shows that bombed. While there are bad shows out there, more often than not, it's just that the show is not a good fit for you. So before your invest all kinds of money and time in a show, do your research. I used the example earlier about how you wouldn't show your high-end semiprecious pieces at the flea market, and though this sounds extreme, it's more common than you might think. Most artists I know have at some point done a show where the vendor next to them was selling sunglasses from China. Make sure you're doing a "handmade" show, no imported machine-made merchandise allowed.

Most states have some sort of guide to fairs and festivals. Search online to get a list, keep your eyes peeled in bead, jewelry, and general craft magazines for advertised shows, or ask around. You'll find some useful resources in the Appendix on page 93. The best time for shows is in the summer or the holiday season.

Evaluating shows

If at all possible, attend the show you're considering as a consumer. Many shows are only annual, so this might mean waiting a whole year to do it, but some are twice a year. And there might be a waiting list anyway, so this will give you plenty of time to get your business together. As you attend the show here are some things to look out for:

* *Is there an admission fee?* Many shows have an outdoor festival format open to the public, but in general having an admission fee is a *good* sign. It means that everyone attending the show is serious about buying. Shows that are free may attract a larger crowd, but they are generally not buying, just killing time or wasting yours. This doesn't mean you shouldn't do free shows; it's just one consideration.
* *If it's a general craft show, notice how many other jewelers are there?* One quarter to one third of the show is a good percentage. It's good to be at a show that is known for having great jewelry vendors, but obviously having too many could be a problem. Notice the price points—are you in the same ballpark?
* *Are people buying?* Do you see cash being exchanged? Are people walking around with bags from purchases? Or are there just a bunch of "looky-loos"?—wording courtesy of my mother.

* *Ask vendors how many years they have been doing the show.* If there are many repeat vendors, that's a good sign. I'll do any show twice because the first one can go wrong for any number of reasons. But if vendors are saying they've come to a show five or six or more years, that's a very good sign.

After checking all these points and getting a good feel for the atmosphere of the show, if it looks like the right fit for you, ask for the on-site office or a coordinator you can speak to about getting into the show next time. Get an application or add your name to the mailing list.

Preparing for your show

So you found a show, you got accepted—congratulations! Now what? Believe me, putting in the serious time and prep work that I'm about to describe is miles more than most artists do, and it will make a huge difference in your success at the show.

I'll talk about booth design and display at length in the next section, but first let's cover some show basics.

Whoever staffs your booth during a show (preferably you) becomes your company image. Your professionalism tells buyers that your company is reliable and a safe place to do business. There are many different elements to consider and put together in trying to gain your customer's business and trust. I will tell you quite honestly that most craft show vendors never even consider the following points, let alone try to perfect them. Remember, making the jewelry is only half of your job. Selling it is the other half, and it takes a conscious effort on your part to make it happen.

Dressing for your show. Be conscious of your attire during a show. It's more than just looking clean and put together. During every show you must

Juried shows

Many shows are juried. All that means is that there is a jury or a panel of people who decide who gets in. This is a sign of a better-quality show. It means that the vendors will meet some quality standards, and that there will be a good mix of different kinds of vendors. Most jurors ask you to submit pictures or slides of your work and make judgments based on what they see. So obviously, high quality photos are important because the nicest jewelry can be rejected just because the photos didn't do it justice.

Christine Lutschg

Like many jewelry artists, Christine Lutschg has focused on selling at shows as a way of showcasing her work and getting it in front of the public. She also has work in several high-end galleries, a rewarding part of her business that lets her artistic, expressive side shine.

But Christine has developed another interesting marketing strategy as well. She stages shows in her home with other artists in different media. Every show rotates artists (except for herself), which keeps them fresh and unpredictable.

Christine creates mostly high-end pieces ranging up to $500 that she says speak to both sides of women. Some are for that fun and funky side, while others are more elegant and sophisticated. Having such an eclectic range means her customers can always find something new and different for themselves or that perfect gift for the hard-to-buy-for. A consistent characteristic, though, is an emphasis on quality—both of materials and craftsmanship.

Christine advises new artists to keep careful track of inventory because it's easy to accumulate quite a lot in a short period of time. But keeping inventory at a minimum and building slowly help an artist keep a better handle on her business, she feels. Because her success has been based on developing repeat customers, she also keeps a very accurate mailing list.

All this attention to detail, both on the creative and the practical side, have helped Christine's business thrive.

Courtesy of Christine Lutschg,
Christine's Designs, Tacoma, WA

wear your jewelry, and whatever piece you're wearing must be for sale. So think about what attire you have that will complement several of your pieces. You're much more likely to sell the pieces your wearing because every design looks better on. It doesn't matter if the tag is hanging down your back—that's a good thing. It's like a walking advertisement for your jewelry. When you sell the piece you were wearing, just put on another one. I tend to wear a lot of neutral, monochromatic clothing so that my jewelry is always the focus.

Know your product. Try to find out everything you can about all the materials in your jewelry. The stones you used, where they're from, and especially the metal in the piece, since that's what people are most likely to ask about. Know if it is sterling, 14k gold, gold filled, or plated. If it is plated, what is the metal underneath? How much nickel is in the piece? Nickel often causes a reaction in people with sensitive skin. You can buy base metal and pewter findings that are made without nickel. Ask your supplier for as much information as possible about the materials you use because customers will want to know.

At my store, we carry a line called Miracle Beads. When we started taking them to shows, I made a sign listing the sizes and prices. Everyone would come up to the booth and ask, "What is a miracle bead?" I would enthusiastically explain, and then the next person would ask the same question, and it happened all day long until not only was my enthusiasm gone, I was downright grouchy. I solved the problem by creating a sign that said "What is a Miracle Bead?" with the entire explanation in a lovely frame.

Now not only did people not ask anymore, but people who probably wouldn't have asked anyway or didn't care found themselves reading the sign out of curiosity. That simple sign also helped sell the product for me when I was busy helping someone else. (By the way, a Miracle Bead is a lucite bead with mirror coating and then a layer of color and then several layers of clear coating so the color reflects off the mirror, giving the bead a miraculous illusion of depth.)

Bottom line, the more you know about your product the better you'll be able to sell it.

Set a sales goal. I just love a goal, especially a sales goal. Many studies have been done about successful businesses, and one thing they all have in common is that the owners were goal setters, both verbally and in writing. I keep a journal for each show (since they all differ) about what worked, what didn't, and how much I sold. I refer to it before doing that show again, and based on the information I've recorded, I set a new goal. I typically look for an increase of at least 15 percent over the last time.

When it's a show I haven't done before, I'll either base my goal on a previous similar show, or I'll figure out how much it's worth for me to be there, taking into consideration the show fee, if I'm paying someone to help me, or if I had to rent tables. One easy rule of thumb is that your show fee should be only 10 percent of your sales. So if your table cost $100, you should plan to do at least $1,000 in sales at that show.

Show manners. Do not sit, eat, smoke, chew gum, or read while working in your booth. You are there to work and to sell. You are paying to be there all day, and the only way you're going to make any money is if you work for it. No matter how good your stuff is, it does not sell itself. Please treat a show experience as if you were behind the counter of your own store, where you surely would not do any of these things. Maybe the smoking, chewing gum, and reading are obvious (though not to all), but let's go over the sitting and eating.

Working at a show is tiring. Standing all day is hard, and maybe you have a bad back. I understand. What I also know is that you're not going to sell as much if you are not making eye contact with the buyer. I promise you if you ever come by my booth at a show my helpers and I are not sitting—ever.

But if you must, there are some solutions. You can raise your table by getting PVC piping cut in 1-foot pieces at the hardware store and sliding them onto the legs of the table. This will raise the table to a comfortable height for your customers. They will notice that they are more comfortable at your booth, though they may not even understand why. The added height allows you to put a stool behind your table. Now you're at eye level with your customer, you are comfortable, and they are comfortable.

The elevated table and seating is especially nice if you plan on working on your jewelry at your booth. "Demo-ing" is very smart because it creates a crowd of people who just stand and watch you. This gives you a chance to chat with them and make that connection. When people have invested so much time, they are more likely to make a purchase, which just attracts more people.

Now back to manners and eating in the booth. You have to eat! If you are lucky enough to get a friend or relative to help out, take advantage and get out of the booth for a quick bite. This will help refresh your body and soul so you're better able to finish the day. However, if you do many shows, the time will come when you'll do one by yourself. (After people have helped you a couple times, the glamour of the whole thing kind of wears off. Turns out shows are actually hard work!) So just bring small protein-rich nutritious snacks to keep under your table and munch throughout the day.

Dealing with knock-offs

People often say "I don't want to make my jewelry at the booth because I'm afraid of someone copying me." I promise you at some point in your jewelry-making career, you will hear someone say, "Oh, I could make that myself." For some reason the person never sees this as rude and sometimes even has the nerve to ask you specifics about the construction of the piece so that they can make it themselves. You can copyright your designs—I'll tell you how on page 89—but my feeling is that worrying about this is a huge waste of your creative energy.

The odds that a person is going to go home, make the exact same piece, show up selling it right next to you at the same show, at the same time, is *zero*. It won't happen. Most likely the person will forget all about it as soon as she leaves your booth. Think about all the cool designs you've seen out and about. How many do you even remember, let alone make? Even if by some crazy coincidence someone did make a piece similar to yours, it wouldn't have your energy in it. By the time someone would even get around to making it, you've moved on to something else.

As a designer, please put your main focus on what you're doing, not what someone else is doing. I used to share a booth with my good friend, Laura Liska. Laura used to make incredible beads out of polymer clay. She made all her own colors, rolled them out super flat, stacked them up in beautiful color sequences, and then sliced them and laid them on the outside of different shapes of polymer beads, creating a bargello effect. They were stunning. You'd have to be incredibly meticulous to do this work. Often, someone would come into our booth and make a comment to Laura such as "Oh, are those Fimo? I could make those." I could never believe my ears. "Are you kidding me? I'd always think. Well, have fun with that!"

What are you supposed to say when someone makes that kind of comment? Well, it's more about how you shouldn't let yourself feel. But I would sincerely say something like, "Oh, do you make jewelry? It's really fun, isn't it? What type of designs do you do?" Let it go, never be rude, because that will come back to bite you. It won't be the last time it happens.

Do not spread a big lunch over your back table and sit down to it as soon as you don't have any customers. Again, this is your store front. You don't see the girls behind the counter at Nordstrom chowing down on some big burrito. It's not professional and it's messy. When I'm hungry I just do a quick duck under the table and pop something in my mouth. Not ideal, but it works. Not being able to have a sit-down lunch is an occupational hazard of the self-employed.

Customer relations

If you are not used to working with the public or are uncomfortable with it, you don't have too many choices—you have to get over it. Maybe someone who has more experience can help you at shows in the beginning until you get the hang of it. Being able to deliver outstanding customer service is not something most of us are born with.

When someone walks up to your table, make eye contact and say hello to let them know you are available to them. Then step back and let them shop. Don't hover—read their body language. You know how annoying it is to be bothered by sales people when you don't want any help. However, as soon as they pick up or touch something, a pair of earrings or some other piece on the table, that is your cue to talk. Say something about that piece, such as, "Oh, I love that pair. I just made them yesterday, that's one of my favorite color combinations . . . , etc." Then they will say something back and you will respond to that and now we are having a conversation—you are making a connection.

It becomes easier over time to talk about your work and yourself as the artist. You will forever be asked questions like, "How did you get started?" "What made you want to make jewelry?" "How long have you been doing this?" and on and on. Eventually the answers will just roll off your tongue.

Working with public has its share of challenges. There will always be people who have had a bad day and decide to take it out on you. Or people who for some reason need to feel more power in their lives by being condescending.

So here's the Oprah part of the book: their problems are not your problems, and no one can make you feel bad unless you let them. Make it your personal challenge to rise above the situation. If someone says "Oh, I can make that," just say back, "That's great. How long have you been making jewelry?" and have a conversation with them. Be as nice as you can. You never want to get a reputation as rude—that will follow you everywhere.

Think of it this way: Your customers are responsible for everything you have—your car, your shoes, your latte—every material thing you own is paid for by your customers, and they pay in exact proportion to how you have treated them—always.

Your customers give you the privilege of pursuing your dreams; they allow you to do what you love by buying your designs. So when you're at a show, remember you are only there because there is a customer on the other side of the table willing to pay you. Without them, you're out of business. It's as simple as that.

Booth display

Because jewelry is so small, you need an enticing and distinctive booth display to show it off. The amount of space you'll have at each show may differ—a six- or eight-foot table? A ten- by ten-foot booth? Or are you sharing with someone so you only have half the space? Whatever it is, you'll need to measure it out for a practice set-up at home. This will give you the opportunity to trouble-shoot and improve your design before the big day.

You'll need to find display props that match the look or style of your jewelry. Art deco? Vintage? Ethnic? Glitzy? Whatever style that you've kept consistent through your business cards and promotional material will play out in your booth display. Think of your allotted area as your own little store front. It doesn't matter that there are a hundred other vendors; your customers should feel as if they are in your own special place of business by the atmosphere you've created.

Table coverings. If you have an entire booth, you'll have to think about fabric or some other material for the back wall and possibly the floor, but whatever your situation, table covers are a given. My approach is to use large covers that conceal table legs and items stored under the table in a color or pattern that coordinates with the colors of my promotional literature. Then I use a smaller, more neutral cloth on the tabletop where my merchandise will be. You can layer as many colors and patterns as you like at different angles for a striking effect.

My friend Laura Liska does beautifully color-coordinated fiber bundles with matching bead kits. All her colors are very earthy and rich. She uses lovely fabric to drape the tables and back wall. She then layers bamboo table runners on top of the fabric. Baskets, dark iron display stands, and wooden frames for signs carry out the rich, earthy look. When you walk up to her table, you really feel as though you've stepped into the loveliest boutique. All this effort equals big sales, since people who seek out one-of-a-kind handcrafts tend to be very visual. They are purchasing based on emotion and connection, so the goal of your booth is to spark that emotion that creates the need to buy.

The props you use don't have to be expensive or fancy, but it is important to add height to the table. If you lay the jewelry out flat, it will easily be missed by people walking by. You only get about ten seconds to catch their attention. Using some props to add height to your display will make it more interesting and will get some of your pieces up at eye level. This can be as simple as covering cardboard boxes with fabric to give height to your table. Be careful not to go too high, though—the average women is only 5'4", so anything above her eye level is wasted.

You can use professional-type jewelry stands (there are references listed in the back), or you can drape your work over just about anything. Use hardware grids or branches to hang earrings, for instance. I often hang my necklaces around lampshades. Cost Plus or Target stores are full of potential display props. Velvet display boards or necklace stands from a display company are not very expensive, but they usually come only in black or white—not the most flattering for a lot of jewelry. You can cover them in different fabrics coordinated to your pieces. Whatever your look, set up your display at home first and make sure it looks great and is easily portable.

Lighting. If your show contract offers an option to purchase electricity, do so. Jewelry is small and you might find yourself in a dark location—the electrical hookup will probably cost only another ten dollars, and it will give you not only lights but possibly a credit card machine (which we'll talk about on page 67).

If you can afford to, I recommend getting Daylights or Ott-Lite brands of flip lamps or clip-on lights. These are full-spectrum lighting, which will show true colors. They are ideal lights for you to design by, but they are also great for your booth. They run anywhere from $40 to $100 apiece and you will need at least two. If that doesn't fit your budget in the beginning, any lights are better than none—regular $10 office clip-on lamps will work.

Show Stopper. A good display has the elements of showmanship: the merchandise is the star, the customer is the audience. Think about featuring one larger piece that I call a "star attraction" or a "show stopper." It may be larger or more expensive than your typical work, though it should be in a kindred style. Display it prominently, make it your centerpiece. The purpose is to catch attention and get folks talking to you, to make that connection. Maybe they aren't in the market for that piece, or maybe they can't afford it, but now they are interested in your work and want a little piece of you, so they buy some earrings or a bracelet.

Shoplifting

Jewelry is small, and it is tempting. You need to be prepared. It's great if the show has visible security guards walking around, but there are things you can do to protect yourself. First, if you have some very expensive items, keep them toward the back of the table close to you. Unless they're worth thousands of dollars, I wouldn't recommend investing in cases, for the simple reason that jewelry shopping is very tactile. People need to touch before they buy. Many times it's just a matter of getting an item into someone's hand before they fall in love with it. If it is under glass, this opportunity may never come. You'd likely lose more in sales than you would lose through shoplifting.

The best preventive for shoplifting is to make eye contact with everyone that walks up to your table and do a quick hello (this is good service anyway). That way they know that you've seen them and are aware of them.

But what if someone does steal? If you didn't see it, there's not much to do. But if you did see it happen, you have every right to say something. I start politely: "I think you have a piece of my jewelry— were you interested in purchasing it?" If you saw them put it into a purse or pocket, you can say, "Oh, I saw it fall in your purse, maybe you didn't notice." Typically, this will cause enough embarrassment that the offender will check where you say you saw it and give it back. That's all we really want, after all. I don't have the energy to call the police and make a huge deal out of it unless it's a repeat offender or a large dollar amount. It's their karma.

Bottom line: try to get your merchandise back, and whether you do or not, report the suspicious person to the show producer or show security so other vendors and security guards will keep their eye on them.

Signage and labeling. Think outside the box when it comes to creating signage for your booth. Imagine, for instance, a beautifully framed tabletop display showing you working in your studio. A matching framed piece could talk about the materials in your jewelry or the technique or style you use. This kind of treatment is attractive, and it can help sell or speak for you when you are busy with other customers. The frames and mats could coordinate with the color and style of your hang tags, earrings cards, and other printed material.

Maybe the most important kind of sign in your booth, though, is one that's often treated as an afterthought—the price tags. Don't you hate it when items aren't clearly marked with the price? Most people won't ask, especially if the salesperson is busy with someone else, or they assume it's too expensive. So think about how you will display prices.

Sometimes labeling each piece individually just doesn't look right, though. For instance, if you have a standing grid holding a lot of earrings cards—to hang a price tag off each one would look tacky and would overwhelm the display. In this case you might give a price range: "Handmade sterling silver and freshwater pearl earrings, $18 to $35."

Interestingly, having your pieces marked with materials and price can actually help sell higher-end items. I don't know about you, but for some reason the more expensive something is, the more I want it! The price can really get someone's attention. You'll hear, "Three hundred dollars? Wow, what kind of stones are these? Rubies, really? I've never seen ruby beads." It can open up a whole new dialogue and appreciation for your work on the part of people who just thought those were red glass.

Logistics

Besides creating a beautiful display, there is the whole business side of a show that needs to be handled smoothly. How professionally you handle each transaction will matter to your customers. If you are clumsy with receipt books, can't add up the sale correctly, get your credit card machine to work, or don't package their purchase nicely, you are fairly sure to lose their future business. This whole process is not as easy as it may look, but planning and practice will make perfect.

The shopping experience. Get some pretty little flat baskets or trays for people to use as shopping carts. Most people will select more than one item once they have started shopping, but if they just use their hands, they will stop shopping as soon as their hands are full. Plus with the jewelry in their hands it may not be visible to you at all times.

Shopping trays do not have to be expensive—just go to Target or Cost Plus. You only need about two or three for the average show. Word of warning: never give your customers paper plates. I've seen this too many times to count—tacky!

The purchasing procedure. After your customer has made her selections, you'll write it up in a two-ply receipt book that you can buy at any office store. One receipt goes to the customer, one stays in the book for your records. Each receipt needs to be marked with your information so the customer can contact you after the sale if she needs to. Stamp them with a rubber stamp, apply an address label, or have some preprinted. That's less expensive than you might think, and you can order as few as five books at a time. I think it's better to use a receipt book and hand-write the sale instead of just using an adding machine receipt, which might be hard to read.

Sales taxes. Anytime you sell to the public, whether at home, at work, or at a show, you must charge the appropriate sales tax for your particular city, county, and/or state. Tax laws vary from state to state, county to county, and city to city, and it's your responsibility to learn the rules. Call your local chamber of commerce or economic development office to get the necessary information.

If you are doing a show out of your area, you will need to get a temporary vendor permit. Generally the promoters of the show will provide the necessary paperwork. After the show, just fill out the form showing your sales and how much sales tax you collected, and then write a check for that amount and send it to the state's Department of Revenue.

The only time you won't be collecting and remitting sales tax will be for wholesale sales because this will generally be to stores who are reselling your pieces, so they are charging and remitting the sales taxes.

Payment—show me the money. How will you get paid? That's the goal, after all, so it deserves some consideration. Cash is good—I'm a fan. But you'll need to be prepared for other methods.

Checks. Personal checks are a reasonable option, too, and even in this day of huge fraud, are fairly safe bets. When you take a check, just verify the ID. Write the driver's license on the check yourself. Never let the customer write it—this is one of the most obvious signs of fraud.

Make sure the check has the printed address and phone number; never take new checks that have not been personalized yet. If you do get a check returned, redeposit it right away, because anyone can make a mistake, miss a deposit, etc. If it is returned a second time, contact the customer and try to work out a way to rectify the situation. The options are for them to send you a cashier's check, to give you their credit card information if you're set up for this, or to return the merchandise.

Make sure to add on whatever fees your bank may have charged you. In most states you can legally add up to a $35 insufficient funds fee, but I will tell you from experience that the more you tack on, the less likely you are to see the money—and really, all you want is what's yours. I would give this process around thirty days. If you still can't collect after that time, send it to a small local collections agency.

This is where having the correct driver's license number on the check is important. Writing bad checks is against the law, and a collections agency can put a lien on the offender's home or a garnishment on their paycheck, and it will show up as a derogatory mark on their credit report until it's taken care of. It won't cost you anything; the collection agency adds their fee onto what the customer has to pay.

All this sounds like a hassle, but I advise you not to let it prevent you from taking checks. You will lose a lot more in sales by refusing them than you will through taking bad checks.

Credit Cards. I would recommend you start taking credit cards when you are doing half a dozen shows or venues a year. It's a lot easier than you might think, and I promise you, it will double your sales. Not because people are debt-happy, but because they just never bring enough cash with them, or they rely on using their debit cards for everything.

You can arrange credit card services through your own bank by inquiring at merchant services. But you don't *have* to use your bank—you should shop around for the best rates. As soon as you receive your business license you will start to receive tons of offers in the mail, but in my part of the country, Costco has the best rates I know of at this time.

You can either buy or lease processing equipment. I recommend leasing in the beginning; normally it's around $20 a month plus a percentage of sales. You will pay anywhere between 2 and 5 percent of the total sale, or more if you have to key the numbers in instead of swiping the card, as would happen in the case of mail order or if the magnetic strip on a card didn't work. The percentage you will be charged is based on your personal credit or Fair Isaac Corporation score (FICO—see www.myfico.com), so shop this around as you would for a loan.

Besides looking for the best rate, be sure to ask how soon the money will appear in the bank after you make a sale. Unfortunately, the money from a sale doesn't actually appear in your bank account for anywhere from 24 to 72 hours—and the sooner it's in the bank, the better.

Packaging. After writing up a sale and getting payment, you'll wrap up your customer's lovely new possessions. This is an opportunity to really make a great impression. Think about your favorite stores, how they wrap things up, what presentation they make. You can use a simple paper or plastic bag, perhaps printed or stamped with your logo, to a treatment that will make a lasting impression—lovely organza, sari bags, or colored tissue and a pretty gift box.

Special packaging can add anywhere from $.50 to $2 of overhead to every sale—a good motivator to make the sale as big as possible. But it can be worth the investment by creating a distinctive image. Go to your local paper or scrap-booking store or look through bag companies online (there are some listed on page 93).

Make sure to include a business card or postcard in the bag. Ask your customer to sign your mailing list, too. Don't just create a random mailing list at the table for anyone to sign—limit it to people who have purchased from you. Be sure to ask for an e-mail address, since sending out e-mails is much cheaper than postcards. Tell them you would like them to sign up so they can receive discounts and private invitations to future show and events.

Then in the future, when you are sending out postcards or e-mails, make sure you have attached a special offer just for those on your mailing list—maybe free admission to a show if you can arrange that, or a free gift with purchase, or 20 percent off any purchase—there are any number of options. This will be more effective than just sending out an announcement about your upcoming show. Don't look at offering discounts as losing money. You'll lose more money through lost sales when people don't show up.

Finally, end every transaction by thanking your customer. This is your last chance to make that personal connection that will encourage them to become a repeat customer. Plus, it's the nice thing to do.

Five. Selling Wholesale

Only after you've done some shows are you ready to approach retail stores. I know many people who do it the other way around because they have a friend who owns a salon or a shop and wants to try to carry some of their jewelry. If you jump right into this, you'll be learning some things the hard way. Why? Because you can't really feel confident that your items will sell at full-mark-up retail prices if you have never sold them at retail yourself.

You need to be able to say to a shop owner, "These are my best sellers, they match up nicely with these other designs, these price points seem to do best for me," and so forth. Only through shows or plenty of at-home parties do you have the experience and knowledge to say that for sure. Why place your work in a store if you're not pretty sure they'll be successful? If they don't do well, the store owner won't reorder. Your goal should be to create long-term business relations with a store.

The fact that a store is very small and not run very professionally does not mean you have to be that way. If transactions are not clear, if they are left up in the air with a "Well, we'll put them out and see how they sell and then we'll go from there,"—that's a no, you're not interested. I know it's a very common conversation all over America, but you would be asking for trouble in getting paid, keeping books straight, and maintaining a healthy future relationship.

I've heard hundreds of horror stories of shops not paying, going out of business, and not returning merchandise or paying for it. You don't have to be a casualty of this phenomenon. You're not that desperate to have your work in a store if it's not all going to be a clean deal. With most professionally run stores, this will not be a problem—in fact, getting quite a few good accounts means doing fewer shows and having more time to stay home to design and do what you love. But it does take some work and time to get there, so let's walk through it.

Basic manners

I carry a lot of finished jewelry in my bead store, so I'm approached by a lot of jewelry artists. Here's a typical experience. Judy Jewelrymaker shows up with her backpack of handmade pieces, walks into the store, and asks to speak to the owner. If she makes it beyond my very inquisitive staff, she will then ask if I want to buy her work. Already she's off on the wrong foot—I don't see anyone without an appointment, and I don't even make an appointment until I've seen a brochure or sample because I don't want to waste anyone's time (especially my own!). Bothering me in the middle of my busy schedule for something I didn't ask for does not put me in a very good frame of mind for purchasing. Everyone is busy. Don't ever just show up anywhere unannounced with your jewelry. The sale won't happen and you won't get a second chance.

Here's a better way, the more professional and effective way to land your work in an appropriate shop or gallery.

Take the time to do some research first. You'll find the right store the same way you found the right show, by checking it out first. Go in and check the other jewelry to see if yours would be a good addition to their selection. Are the price points in the same range? How would yours stand out? Talk to some of the sales people. Be wearing some of your jewelry. Tell them you're a local artist and ask which pieces are doing best for them. Ask for the buyer's contact information. Then go home and give him or her a call. You could also make contact by e-mail, but you'll fair better with a phone call.

Tell the buyer that you were in her store earlier, how much you loved it, and that you are a local jewelry artist whose jewelry could be a good fit. Then ask when they will be open to buy or when they will be looking at new artists. This is so much less invasive than, "Can I show you my jewelry," and puts less pressure on the buyer. Remember, half the sale is the relationship and store buyers are just like anybody else—they would rather buy from people they like and enjoy doing business with. We're trying to possibly build something long-term here.

Now the buyer can answer with, "I've already bought through the season, but contact me again in the summer." Or she may say, "I'm looking all the time." In any case, ask if you can send them your portfolio. No one says no to that. Send it off, put a little handwritten note inside thanking her for taking the time to look at your work and promising to contact her soon. Then after about a week, drop a call or an e-mail to see if she has received it and if she has any questions. Is she interested in setting up an appointment? If not, ask when she would like you to contact her again. Whatever it is, one month or three or six, make a note to yourself and then do it.

The appointment

At some point you will have the appointment. A fundamental thing you have to decide is whether you will go in with one-of-a-kind pieces that can be selected and maybe even paid for on the spot, or whether you will have representative samples and will take an order. Either approach can work. Long-term, though, having samples with a catalog to facilitate reorders will potentially result in more consistent business.

When going to the appointment—be on time! I'm amazed at how many people do not think of it as rude to keep others waiting. You'll also want to design a way to show your work that's both attractive and portable. Many people use a type of jewelry roll, or display pads with loops and snaps that many pieces can be attached to. These work, but I would encourage you to think outside the box a little. Use jewelry pads or stands that you've covered with a lovely fabric or put bracelets and earrings in gift boxes or pretty bags.

One jewelry maker I met with opened his backpack and started taking out all these lovely satin bags tied with organza ribbons. They were in beautiful colors—magenta, royal blue, emerald green—I was so excited by the presentation, and I hadn't even see the jewelry yet! This is the mood you want to put the store buyer in when she's meeting with you.

To be clear and business-like, be sure that everything is priced, preferably with your wholesale prices. Let the buyer know what your minimum dollar order is, too. I consider $200 a rock-bottom minimum. Have an order form handy, preferably two-ply so you can give her a copy, or write up the order on your laptop if you're set up for that.

Questions you should be prepared to answer

Question: What is your turnaround time, or, when will this order be ready? Maybe the buyer needs delivery by October 15th for the Christmas season, or maybe she wants it as soon as possible.

Wrong answer: It will be ready tomorrow. I know you're very excited and want to go home and make it all right now, but I caution against this. Instead, follow this basic principle: under-promise, over-deliver.

Right answer: Even if you think you can get it done in a week, tell her two. If you have to order some materials that may take an extra week, tell her four. Whatever you think you can do, double it. She's not going to cancel the order—she just wants you to be honest and realistic. If you do get it done early, you can call and say, "I have that order done ahead of schedule. Do you want it delivered now or when we originally discussed?" This makes you look so good.

To tell the truth, I would faint if that ever happened to me even one time. I have had an artist promise me a month and then call nine months later—did I still want the order? Do I reward bad service? No. This artist lost my business forever. Give yourself more time because life happens. You get sick, your kids get sick, you can't get the materials, things happen that you can't control. Most people are forgiving, but not over and over again, so why put yourself in a position to disappoint?

*

Question: How will you get paid? Many store owners want to pay what's called "net 30," meaning they will pay you thirty days from the date of the finished order or the date on the invoice you present them, not the order date. That means you have to pay for your materials out of your pocket and cover the time it takes to create the jewelry and then wait a full month before you get any money.

Answer: Tell the buyer that her first order is COD (cash on delivery). This can be paid by check or by credit card. Maybe subsequent orders can be net 15, but your best protection is to always require COD. If you can't deliver the order in person, you can send items COD through the post office, Federal Express, or UPS. My experience has been that Fed Ex is the fastest and most reliable. Yes, it's the most expensive, but using it is perfectly acceptable protocol.

Requiring COD will not offend a buyer. She'll probably ask for net 30 just to see if she can get it. But don't feel that you have to give it—just be prepared to say how you want to be paid. The unfortunate truth is that many stores don't pay on time, so you'll be smart not to offer terms until you've reached a level of financial stability.

To initiate a terms arrangement with a shop or gallery, you'll ask for their trade reference sheet—all legitimate businesses have one. Call these references to find out how quickly they pay on their accounts. It's important to go through this exercise because when you offer terms, stores will generally spend more because it's on credit.

What if a store doesn't pay on time? I normally give our accounts a two-week-grace period, after which I call them and send another copy of the invoice. (Many people will claim they didn't receive it or must have lost it, which might actually be true.) Just be persistent with the phone because the squeaky wheel will get the grease. Not that you have to be obnoxious—you can be polite *and* persistent.

*

Question: Will you do trade-outs? Meaning if a piece doesn't sell, will you trade it back for something else? This is not a terribly common question, but I do want you to be prepared for it should it come up.

Answer: Of course anything that breaks can be returned for replacement, but we're talking here about items that just didn't sell. Perhaps you'll be willing to do it one time or during the first six months while you're establishing a relationship. Be clear that it's not your ongoing policy, though. To take returns or trade-outs long-term means you're effectively selling on consignment, which we'll talk about next.

Consignment

Just about every jewelry artist I know has placed work on consignment at some point in her career. I would recommend you find a consignment store the same way you would find a show or other venue, by going into it and making sure it's the right fit for your jewelry. This is especially important in a consignment shop because they won't actually pay for anything until it sells. So if it's the wrong place for your jewelry, you'd be wasting your time and their space and missing other opportunities to make an actual sale.

If a store looks right and feels right, and you're willing to take the risk, ask about its consignment policy. Any professional consignment store will have a contract you can read over. You'll want to see what the percentage is first thing. When I first started in this business, consignment percentages were typically 50/50—that is, I got half of what the store owner got. Nowadays it's more likely to be 70/30 (meaning 30 percent for you, 70 percent for the store), or 60/40. Here are some important questions to ask:

Question: How often will you get paid? Most stores pay once a month. Find out how they keep track of their (your) inventory and if you get a copy of that each month with your check.

Question: Do you have access to your jewelry whenever you want? Can you get it out for a weekend if you have a big show? Can you help with any of the display? Give the store as much information about your jewelry as possible—postcards, informational signage—because once it's out of your hands, you don't have any control or influence over how it's being sold.

Question: What about theft? This should be in your contract. Most stores will not claim responsibility for theft, but you should still ask this question so you will know the policy.

We used to have a small tray of sterling silver and stone pendants on our counter at the cash desk. They were all on consignment from my good friend Jessica of Jess Imports. One day someone put the whole tray in her purse and I never noticed until she was gone. I ended up paying for them even though we had no contract, mostly because I was raised Catholic and naturally carry a lot of guilt! But also because I felt it was the right thing to do, and I wanted to keep a good relationship with Jessica, both personally and professionally. This is not something you can expect, though.

To sum up, like any decision, there are pros and cons of consignment. The main argument against it is that you will have to wait until a piece sells to get paid. But there's also the risk that it could sit there quite a while when you could be showing it and selling it somewhere else. The pros would be: getting a regular check every month (assuming pieces have been selling), and the store will probably take more inventory than they would of if they had to buy outright. A consignment arrangement also gives you an opportunity to test-market new, maybe more expensive designs without much risk or investment on the part of the buyer.

Sales reps

What is a sales rep, or representative? It's someone who might start looking very attractive to you when the glamour of shows and beating down doors has worn off. A sales rep's job, by definition, is someone who represents several different artists. Sales reps will only represent artists who have samples to reorder from, not one-of-a-kind artists. Most sales reps specialize in one category of product—in your case, someone who reps jewelry and/or accessories.

Established sales reps know and have regular appointments set up with store buyers. When she sees them she will show them her new artists' samples and take orders. The order will then be faxed or e-mailed to you; you fill the order and ship the goods. When you get paid, you in turn will pay the sales rep 15 percent of that order's total. In calculating your pricing, this will count as part of your overhead, not as an add-on expense. Your rep did all the work to get the order—you just had to fill it.

Many sales reps display at national gift shows. Every major city from Seattle to Miami has a gift show. These shows are mostly attended by store owners and buyers. You have to have a business license to get in, so they are not open to the public and are wholesale only. Reps get booths at these shows and put up all the samples from the artists they are representing. Not many artists can afford to do these shows, even the ones in their own hometown, because they are very expensive. But because the reps are doing them all over the country, you get an unlimited opportunity to place your jewelry in stores and galleries that would otherwise never see your work.

How do you find a rep? If you have been working with store buyers, you can ask them for recommendations. Or you can attend the gift show yourself by showing your business license. You'll be able to spot the jewelry reps by their booth design, which usually has many different sections or panels of what looks like the work of different artists. You can also check in the show office, which should have bulletin boards listing "Reps looking for lines." Or you can post a "looking for reps" notice yourself.

When you find a likely rep, you'll want to interview him or her and get a list of references because it is essentially like hiring an employee.

You need to really have your business together before you make a commitment to work with a rep. That means solid designs, reliable resources for your materials, and a shipping/fulfillment system in place to get orders out efficiently. It's not a step to take because you think the money will just start rolling in. It's a lot of work. You have to produce on time, and an unexpected big order could knock you for a loop. There will not be many reorders if you can't perform your end of the agreement.

But I know many artists who have worked with one or more reps to increase their business tremendously and get fantastic national exposure. It can really be an exciting option when you're ready.

eBay

I can't possibly discuss venues for selling your jewelry with out mentioning eBay. Not because I'm endorsing it, but because I get asked about it all the time. I'm going to cover doing your own website later, but eBay is different. You post your jewelry and folks bid on it. You set the starting bid (your bottom price), and then you wait. If you're a total introvert who never wants to leave the house or meet the public, it's an opportunity to put your work into the market. But let me just say this: Bloomingdale's is not looking for their next jewelry designer on eBay.

eBay provides extensive tools to help potential customers set up their own stores.

To be fair, though, let's just stick with the facts (though that was one). There are about 20,000 pieces of jewelry listed on eBay at any given time, so it's highly saturated. High-end jewelry does not sell as well as less expensive work, most likely because people can't actually judge the quality on their computer screen.

If you want to give eBay a try, here are some tips:

* Take extremely good photos.
* Write very detailed descriptions.
* Create an eBay store (the site offers an instructional kit for doing this).
* Have a lot of inventory. People who do best have literally hundreds of pieces on at one time.
* Realize that this is best considered as "extra" income. It takes time to build a virtual clientele across the country.
* Create an extremely clear and generous return policy. This is not like craft shows where buyers see the merchandise before they buy. This is someone buying based on a photo and description and possibly your reputation. If they are disappointed with the quality or thought your descriptions were not accurate, you need to rectify the situation quickly to keep your reputation on eBay as a good person to do business with. People post their experiences on each transaction you have, so many people will buy based on your customer service feedback.

eBay, of course, charges a fee for its services and takes a percentage of each sale. It's easy to get payment through their PayPal system, which I understand you can even arrange credit card services through.

Six. Marketing

This is a short discussion about a big subject. A lot of what we've talked about already is really marketing—how you identify your customer, how you position your product line, how you brand your business through the venues you choose and the look you develop. It's all marketing, really. But here are some specific marketing activities that will help create sales opportunities for you.

Advertising

As an artist, you won't often find that purchasing print or broadcast advertising pays off. Your best advertising will come from word of mouth. Consider the money you spend on making postcards, brochures, and portfolios your advertising budget, since that is essentially what all your promotional material is about.

If you do get an opportunity to do some group advertising for a show program, or if a bigger show is running ads and asking any the exhibitors if they want to pay to be featured in the ads, this might be something to consider. If you do advertise in a show program, it's smart to attach some kind of offer, discount, or free gift to direct attendees to your booth. It also helps you track sales, which in turn will help you judge the effectiveness of the ad for future decision-making.

Your website

It has become essential for even the smallest business to have a Web presence. You will be surprised how many people will ask you as you start out, "Do you have a website?" as if it's the easiest thing in the world to build and maintain.

True, is easier than it's ever been, with more help available than ever before. But it's still a significant investment of either time or money. Personally, I would rather pay someone than learn how to do it myself because I need to focus on the areas where I have the most talent and aptitude. You may have a real affinity for computers and the Internet, though, so it's up to you whether to design, build, and maintain your own site or hire someone to do it for you. But I'm not the one to tell you how, and doing it is far beyond the scope of this book.

There are plenty of freelance Web designers out there that charge by the hour, and they're easy to find. Put the word to your friends, and you'd probably find someone with a son who is a webbie. Check out some local retailers' websites and find out who did them. Contact your chamber of commerce. When you get a lead, look at other work they have done and check with the business they did the work for. Were they on time? Easy to work with? Then get an hourly quote to build the site and a cost schedule for maintaining it.

Why have a website? I think every artist needs at least a one-page website, the same as they should have business cards and postcards. On the other hand, I don't think it's likely that you will ever need to set it up as an online merchant with a shopping cart and shipping services, because jewelry is very tactile. People need to see it and touch it in person to fall in love enough to buy it. Plus everyone's computer screen shows the colors differently.

Having said that, every year I pay very close attention to what the experts are saying after each holiday season, how it went for retailers, what were the big items, how big the sales increases of the big-box retailers, and so forth. I'm very in to all the business news. The biggest increase this past year? Online sales. Biggest product increase online? Jewelry. So maybe we're changing. Maybe the Web is the market of the future for jewelry makers. As I mentioned before, there are currently almost 20,000 pieces of jewelry on eBay at any given time, and I'm sure that's bound to keep increasing.

Getting started. All that being said, this is what I think you need on your website, at least to start:

Robin Renzi, Me&Ro

Robin Renzi started making jewelry when she was a sophomore in high school. She became enamored of jewelry at a very young age, influenced by her Italian grandmother and her mother. Its cultural significance, the beauty of stones from the earth, the timelessness all appeal to her. This is a passionate woman, inspired by the place jewelry holds in our lives, from the first ring from a boyfriend, to a necklace from a best friend, or a special piece from an aunt or uncle or grandmother. She feels that jewelry holds memories and becomes part of our life stories, and her pieces are notable for the use of symbols and words.

Robin began designing collections with the inception of Me&Ro in 1991. The first store she approached was Barney's in New York—her favorite—and she felt the collection would work well there. Today, Me&Ro pieces can be found at Nordstrom and Neiman Marcus, among others. Prices range from $100 to $30,000, and the typical customer is looking for well-made, meaningful, timeless, and original work.

Me&Ro has had a high profile, being featured in many magazines and on a star cast of celebrities. A big jolt to the business when it was only eight years old was having Julia Roberts find their work and wear a piece in her hit movie, *Knotting Hill*. She became a real fan of Me&Ro, and her publicist got the work placed in popular magazines. The kind of word-of-mouth attention this led to is priceless.

Robin's best advice, though, is to make the jewelry itself the primary focus. "Do not think about success, or whether anyone will like what you're doing. Follow your own creative process and be true to it," she says. "Once you find your own original voice, then you need a plan." She notes the importance of recognizing your limitations and playing to your strengths. Can you sell your product, write a business plan? Can you wear fifty different hats and run a business? "Sadly," she says, "talent is not enough. You must also learn the art of business. Business is tough, and I think that's why most artists fail. There is a lot of marginal work out there, because most talented people do not know how to sell and market their work. So we as a society are left with a lot of bad product and no choices.

"You have to fight the good fight with integrity and discipline—it's not easy, but someone has to do it!" she concludes.

Courtesy of Robin Renzi, Me&Ro, Los Angeles, CA

* *Opening page.* Name of the company, your name, a picture of you if you want, your contact information, a picture or two of your jewelry. Then—and this is important—250 words about your jewelry. Include information and buzz words: sterling silver, gold filled, handcrafted, specific stone names, Austrian crystal, contemporary styling.

  Add links to other pages on your site. Why? Because when people do searches online, the search engines only search the opening pages of websites. Why 250 words? That's currently the minimum to be picked up by all the big search engines. So talk it up!

* *A page listing where your work can be found*—stores or galleries, with links to their pages.

* *A page listing your show schedule*—where to see you in person or how to make an appointment.

* *A page with your biography or resume.* This can be the same information as in your portfolio.

* *One or more gallery pages with pictures of your work.* Include some pages with your newest pieces, and then some that show your complete collection. Here, you can list retail prices and suggest that stores contact you for wholesale pricing information.

* *A one-page order form* that can be printed out and either faxed or mailed to you.

* *A Press Room of one or more pages,* including press clippings, or events you've been a part of.

A website with all these features will not just get you started, but should be all you'll need for quite a while. Have it updated about once a month. Write a new opening page each month so that return visitors have something new to look at.

If you are featuring items for sale with prices and you're having people call to purchase or using your order form, you'll definitely want to update your inventory list often. Invite people to sign up for an online newsletter or at least for notification of updates. Each time you change designs you can send out an e-mail blast to let your list know or invite them to private events.

Networking and community involvement

Don't miss opportunities to meet new artists and get involved with artists groups. Maybe the area your home is in (where your business license is based) is actually considered a business district. If so, it's likely to have a business meeting every month focused on ways to attract more business to the area. Even though you may not open your home for business, this is a great way to find out what others in your community are doing and get your business known.

Does your district have a local summer or holiday festival? Normally these are run by volunteers. Get involved; your business could be featured as a sponsor, or you could be the contact for the press and get a chance to plug your business for free. Most cities of any size have art centers where there are classes or meetings. Offer to teach or lecture. When you are involved with a festival that offers workshops, sign up for some just to meet people or offer to demonstrate your craft. This might get your work featured in the press packets for the event.

Start making donations for charity auctions. Keep an eye out for when they are advertised in the paper and get the contact information. Tell them you're a local jewelry artist and would love to donate a piece for their auction. You can write off the donation and it will give you tons of exposure. Most likely the cost of the necklace will be cheaper than any ad you could have placed.

The sponsoring group will let you put out postcards or business cards. They will probably ask you each year after that, and lots of other groups may start asking too, since every auction always needs more donors. You can turn down some if it gets to be too many. But it's great exposure, especially if your price ranges are toward the high end, since this is generally the customer who attends and bids on these types of items. You will probably end up with quite a few calls, especially if you are in attendance yourself and get a chance to talk yourself up.

You'll find endless opportunities to get involved in art communities, local or even national. Attend a national event just to take some classes or seminars and meet new people. When you attend a large bead event, you may be there to buy and take classes, but go to all the social activities, too. You are bound to meet other artists and glean loads of information. You will never be sorry you invested time and money to attend these shows, including mine, The Puget Sound Bead Festival (shameless plug).

The press release

You can attract attention all on your own if your business is doing something out of the ordinary or something for charity. A press release informs the media of your special announcement or event.

Every small town (and large) has its own paper that has to be filled with news every day. This could be your day. At the very least they can put a notice in the community calendar for free. But you never know—they could be having a slow news day and think, "Hey, what about that group of women artists story?" and give you a call. Next thing you know there's a whole feature story on you. You put copies of it in your portfolio and on your website, and pretty soon every boutique in town will want to carry that new hot artist. It's all possible from a simple press release. It's happened to me and my business many times over. But it has to be newsworthy, not just a sale. Make it short and simple is best; too long, and it won't get read. Just who, what, when, where, and why—and that's it.

Here's a sample press release

March 1st, 2006
FOR IMMEDIATE RELEASE

Local artists to help Mothers Against Violence

Five Tacoma jewelry artists will be holding an exhibition of their latest work on Friday, March 10th, in the lobby of the Tacoma Sheraton from 12 to 5 PM to support the Tacoma Mothers Against Violence group. Twenty percent of all sales of their new sring collection of jewelry will go directly to supporting MAV. Local city counsel member Sharon McGavick will be introducing the show and speaking about her involvement with MAV from 12 to 1 PM. For more information, contact Viki Lareau at (253) 572-5529.

* * *

You can also send updates of what you are doing as an artist to national art magazines. They always are doing feature stories on artists. Pick up a bunch of magazines such as *Ornament* or *The Crafts Report*, next time you're in Barnes & Noble. Find out how to submit your story (many magazines have writer guidelines on their websites), brush up those writing skills, and send your best pictures. If you really persevere, you'll learn what it takes, and you'll get the coverage. Stories about you and your work are priceless; you can't buy the kind of attention and credibility they give you.

Seven. Managing the Business

The following activies are definitely not why I'm in the business of beads and jewelry. Some people love the nitty gritty aspects; I'm not one of them. To me, doing these fundamental business chores is like doing dishes. It has to be done, so you might as well be thorough and efficient and get it over with.

Obtaining a business license

Getting a business license is one of the first things you'll do when you've committed to the idea of being in business. Once you have it you'll be able to buy at wholesale discounts, set up a bank account, and get into shows. I really discourage those who try to stay "under the radar" as long as possible because they want to avoid the paperwork. It's not that much paperwork for a small single-person business, and furthermore, it's illegal.

Every city and state has different requirements and costs. But most licenses are very inexpensive, and some are even free. You can go to www .departmentofrevenue.org and click on your state to find out the requirements, or call your state's department of revenue. This is the first license you'll need to get. It's also called your UBI number or "tax" number.

Your city may require a separate business license, too. Contact your local tax and license office and ask. I would just be honest about what you need or go in there and have them set you up. Having a home-based business may require some additional licenses as well. Getting these is a one-time effort; it's not expensive, and it makes you legitimate—congratulations!

One of the forms will probably ask you to project your sales for the upcoming year, which will determine whether you'll be required to report sales monthly or quarterly. Go on the low side for now; reporting quarterly should be fine for at least the first couple years.

Filing taxes

Filing taxes at year-end is fairly simple for a home-based business. Normally all that's required is a "Schedule C" profit or loss statement from the business. The rumor on the street is that if you don't show a profit or at least show you're making a good attempt to make one after three to five years, they can take your license away because it looks like a hobby that you're doing to get a tax break instead of a real business.

Unless you love doing taxes and are very good at keeping up with all the updates, I would recommend hiring an accountant, even though you'll have only limited need for one. I only go to mine once a year at tax time, but it's worth every penny. I wouldn't dream of fixing my own car, cutting my own hair, or installing our new dishwasher or any of the others hundreds of things I don't know how to do. I put my energy into the things that only I can do, and I still don't have enough time, so I can't imagine tackling tasks I don't know how to do. They would actually end up costing more if I did it myself because my time is not free. As I've said before, I'm a big fan of hiring professionals.

Banking

As soon as you obtain your business license you'll want to get a business checking account. Mixing up business with your personal finances is a recipe for disaster. Go to the bank you're currently using if you're happy there and see someone in merchant services. More than likely they'll suggest that you to open a DBA ("doing business as") account. Your checks will be printed with your name followed by DBA and your business name.

Ask for a debit card and/or a credit card to be attached to this account. You'll especially need these if you're doing any traveling on your company time. Your checks will also give your business more credibility with suppliers and vendors. They can act as additional ID for shows that require more than just your business license to get in, too.

Inventory

You'll need two inventory systems, one for the loose materials and components you buy and one for your finished pieces. Anything that works for you is fine, you just need to find something that you will use. It can be fish tackle boxes, ziplock bags, craft organizers, drawers, jars, whatever. For the loose materials, label each container with what the product is, how much it cost per piece (or foot, inch, or gram), and where you got it, and possibly a stocking number so you can reorder it if you need to. Once you have a system in place, whenever you buy product, come home and record the cost immediately while that information is still fresh and you know where the receipts are. Make a filing system for those receipts and invoices, too. You'll be looking up product very often to recheck prices or to reorder.

Your inventory of finished pieces needs to be documented, too, especially if they are one-of-a-kind pieces. The simplest way is to take digital photographs and store them on your computer (but be sure to keep backups!). You can even scan the pieces or lay them on a photocopier. Many times I'll make something, sell it, and then forget what it looked like, which makes it pretty hard to duplicate. You really need to keep an archive of your designs.

The jewelry designer manager software I mentioned on page 50 has a place for inventorying all your loose components and finished jewelry, too.

The Small Business Administration

I just want to mention this fantastic organization briefly because it can be a tremendous resource while you're building your business. Every major city has an SBA office. It has plenty of free materials and very affordable seminars on such subjects as writing a business plan, financing, and marketing to help with the logistics of your business.

The SBA also has a great program called SCORE. This is a group of retired business people who volunteer to mentor new business people. The SBA matches you up with someone who has done what you are trying to do—perhaps a retired artist in your area. You can meet as often as you like free of charge. I used a representative from the SCORE program at least four times over the first couple years of my business and found the help to be invaluable.

Protecting your work

You may recall from my earlier diatribe how I feel about protecting your work against knockoffs. To me, it's just not very important. But I realize you might not feel that way, and your position is perfectly legitimate. So here's a very short course in how to get copyright protection for your designs.

First, the moment you put your work out to the public, if it is original, it is automatically protected by common law copyright. In fact, all you have to do is make a sketch of your idea or take a photo of a piece you've just made. Put a copyright notice on it (one of those little c's in a circle), along with your name and the date, just to be extra cautious. Voila! Your work is protected. Up to a point.

If you want extra protection, for instance in case somebody copies your work and begins to sell it as their own, and you think you would want to start some legal proceedings against them, then file for an official copyright on your work.

This is simple: Go to www.copyright.gov, download the application, and send it in with a $30 fee. Your copyright registration will then be on record in case you ever find yourself in a position to need it.

Design patents—that is, protection for a design that is completely unique and unusual to the point of not being like anything else in how it's made, or how it looks, or how it's used—is more expensive, complicated, and slow. You'll probably need the help of a patent attorney and a few thousand dollars. And you have only a year from the time your work is first presented to the public in which to apply for a design patent.

Work ethics

I'm not talking about how hard you work or how much time you put in. I'm talking about what's okay to borrow from others and what's not okay. This is definitely a hot issue, and open to a lot of perspectives and opinions. That's why it's so challenging to make hard and fast rules around it. A designer's perspective would be different from a teacher's, from a shop owner's, or from a student's.

But here is a way to think about it: If you take a class to learn a certain peyote beaded bracelet, can you turn around and make more and sell them or teach that bracelet to someone else for profit? No, not and claim it as your own original design. You may sell or teach that technique, but you must change the project or end result. Basic techniques are taught and shared all the time— wirework, PMC, pearl knotting, peyote stitch. You can't copyright a technique. However it is definitely unethical to sell or make the exact same project as another artist's and present it as your own original idea.

That being said, my own perspective as a shop owner is probably different than the designer who considers her work to be her "art." I am the first person to admit that I use designs out of Neiman Marcus or Sundance catalogs to inspire new project ideas for our store classes, because my customers want to learn to make what's popular now. Do I ever claim them as my own original ideas? No! In fact, part of the sales pitch is that a student can make a piece just like what you can buy out of the latest fashion magazines.

Other teachers might have a different opinion. They work hard to develop their classes and are very protective of them. My mindset (because I am a teacher also) is that once you have taught a project, you've put it out in the world. You have decided to let others make it, and what they do with it from then on is their business. But it is still unethical for a student to claim it as their original design or to teach it as their own for pay.

Handouts are protected by the copyright laws. I honestly would never care if someone else teaches one of my classes, because it's not "me" teaching—so it's not the same. However I wouldn't want someone to copy my handouts and present them as their own. The distinctions are subtle, but I'll bet you "get" them. In general it is always just better to come up with your own ideas anyway, which will get easier the more you try.

When I was starting out, I was often guilty of looking to see what others were doing and trying to do something similar, because I must not have felt secure enough in my own talent. That time is past, and now I avoid knowing what others are designing or teaching so I can develop completely fresh ideas.

I hope that my company can inspire other shops and designers, like so many did for me. Inspiring and sharing our thoughts and ideas can only further this craft. The ultimate goal for everyone should be to keep beaded jewelry popular so we all can prosper.

Conclusion

I hope that this book has helped you decide if a career as a jewelry designer is for you. Maybe you are excited about your new endeavor, or completely overwhelmed by the journey in front of you, or maybe you're feeling a combination of the two. Maybe you have decided selling your jewelry is not for you, and you'd rather just continue beading as your favorite hobby. All these are positive decisions. It has been absolutely my privilege to be a part of your path. Helping and observing people's lives change because of beads and jewelry making is my favorite part of this business and my greatest reward.

I hope that you find that, too—no matter where your interests take you. It's exciting to watch dreams and passions come alive when we put our own pure creative energy into them. I mostly hope this book will help your talent (and bank account!) sparkle as brightly as your beads!

> *If we did all the things we are capable of doing,*
> *we would literally astound ourselves.*
>
> **—Thomas Edison**

Craft Fairs and Festivals Sites

www.castleberryfairs.com Clearinghouse for upcoming art and craft fairs and craft galleries, includes show calendar, applications, and exhibitor information for New England region.

www.festivalnet.com Source for art and craft shows, music festivals, home shows, and specialty events in the U.S. and Canada.

www.sugarloafcrafts.com Upcoming show schedule for the juried Sugarloaf Art and Craft Festivals; resources for handcraft artists.

www.jolaf.com Juried arts and crafts festivals contact listings; links to applications for 500 festivals; searchable database.

www.artandcraftshows.net Search for arts and crafts shows by festival or fair, dates, city, state, or region; national and regional listings.

www.craftmasternews.com A show guide for artists, crafters, and vendors for craft shows in the western states, covering AZ, CA, CO, ID, KS, MT, ND, NE, NM, NV, OK, OR, SD, TX, UT, WA, and WY. Show listing, vending guide, subscription to print publication.

www.smartfrogs.com *Art and Craft Show Yellow Pages* is a regional show guide/directory for craftsmen artists, food vendors, and resellers in CT, MA, NH, NJ, NY, PA, RI, VT, DE, MD,VA; subscriber-only access.

www.craftshowplace.com/craftfairs Resource for crafters to exhibit at top forty craft fairs and art shows in the country. List of top 900 shows available for purchase.

www.craftsfaironline.com Claims to be the "Oldest And Largest Craft Directory On The Web"; offers links to craft shows and events, supplies and materials, craft publications, software, and projects.

www.artsandcrafts.about.com Information and links to thousands of craft shows, fairs, festivals, and events.

www.fairandfestivals.com Comprehensive listing of several art and craft websites with provided links.

Display and Packaging Resources

www.jewelrydisplay.com Wholesale distributors of jewelry displays, boxes, jewelers' tools and supplies.

www.storefixtures2000.com Online retailer of store display fixtures, providing store design and planning assistance; will build custom display cases, counters, and other display products.

www.displays2go.com Offers trade show displays and custom fabricated displays; product line includes over 5,100 different display stands, display racks, trade show display booths, banner stands, and store fixtures.

www.ajdny.com Advanced Jewelry Display specializes in wholesale and retail lines of jewelry display cases.

www.minikitz.com Online retailer of small jewelry and display kits, dressing table size.

www.kassoy.com/index Online retailer with extensive list of tools and supplies for the jeweler trades.

www.swalter.com Online retailer for bags, boxes, bows, wrapping paper, gift packaging, and retail and shipping accessories.

www.crispak.com Designs, prototypes, and produces displays, corrugated packaging, retail package designs, and retail store displays.

www.makeyouhappy.com American Retail Supply specializes in packaging materials for retail stores; spectrum reaches from clear poly bags and jewelry boxes to tissue paper and shrink wrap.

www.bagsandbowsonline.com Online vendor of retail packaging products, accessories, and seasonal products.

aajewelry.readyflexgo.net The jeweler's "supermarket" sells equipment and supplies, jewelry boxes, and displays.

Small Business Resources

www.entrepreneur.com Entrepeneur's resource with step-by-step details for starting a business, creating a home office, business finance solutions, and e-commerce information.

www.businessweek.com/smallbiz Small business news, advice, and resources from BusinessWeek online.

http://sbs.smallbusiness.yahoo.com Resources for starting a business, including sales and marketing, online business, legal and financial.

www.allbusiness.com Bills itself as the champion of small business. Offers business advice, buyer's guides, directories, breaking news, and a business glossary.

www.sba.gov Website of the United States Small Business Administration, offers tips on starting, financing, and managing a small business.

www.sba.gov/financing/special/women Website of the United States Small Business Administration, with information specific to women entrepreneurs; features online women's business center.

www.womanowned.com Business network for women that offers information, tools, networking opportunities, and advice for starting a business; includes searchable list of woman owned business.

www.4expertise.com/women-ressources Business resources for women with extensive listing of associations and help links.

www.proposalwriter.com/small General resources for small, minority, and women-owned businesses, offering links to procuring governments grants, business plans and proposals, and small business innovation research.

www.score.org/women SCORE "Counselors to America's Small Business." A source of free and confidential small business advice for entrepreneurs, a resource partner with the U.S. Small Business Administration.

www.count-me-in.org Website of Count-Me-In, a nonprofit organization committed to increasing and strengthening women's economic opportunities; provides loans and business resource links.

www.craftcouncil.org Website of the American Craft Council provides listing of shows and markets and an extensive database of library and craft resources.

Promotional Printers and Resources

www.modernpostcard.com Provides direct mail advertising for businesses.

www.megacolor.com Producer of four-color sell sheets, catalogs, and postcards.

Publications

www.craftsreport.com Online edition of *The Crafts Reports* magazine, a monthly business magazine for the crafts professional; provides discussion board, industry information, artist and show finder, and listing of national craft organizations.

www.beadworkmagazine.com A great complement to *Beadwork* magazine, this online edition offers browsers free projects, an extended calendar of bead-related events, galleries of readers' work, back issues and beading books, and much more.

Beading Books

Beader's Stash by Laura Levaas
Bella Beaded Jewelry by Donatella Ciotti
The Bead Directory by Elise Mann
The Beader's Companion by Judith Durant and Jean Campbell
Stringing Style by Jamie Hogsett
Visit www.interweave.com for a complete list of beading books.

Helpful Miscellaneous Websites

www.wholesalecrafts.com Online network connecting independent artists with retail businesses that sell arts and crafts.

www.jewelrydesignermanager.com Offers easy-to-use Jewelry Designer Manager™ soft-ware, books, and accessories to help you manage your jewelry business.

www.gem.net Extensive online gem resource with complete library, current events, and gem excursion offers.

www.intergem.com International gem and jewelry show website; complete show schedule and event listings, and exhibitor information.